Phonics

Susan Hill

Stenhouse Publishers
York, Maine

Stenhouse Publishers, P.O. Box 360, York, Maine 03909
www.stenhouse.com

ISBN 1-57110-326-0

First published in 1999
Eleanor Curtain Publishing
906 Malvern Road
Armadale Vic 3143
Australia

Production by Publishing Solutions
Edited by Ruth Siems
Designed by David Constable
Printed in Singapore

Contents

Introduction
In/tro/duc/tion

Phonics is instruction about the relationship between sounds and letters. Phonics involves understanding the alphabetic principle, which is the idea that spoken language is made up of sounds, and sounds can be mapped to written letters. In the English language, a letter or combination of letters represents sounds. For example, in the word 'luck' there are four letters and three sounds because 'ck' represents a single sound. Knowing about phonics is necessary in order to provide clear, explicit information for children to use in reading and writing. Knowledge of where phonics fits in reading and writing enables teachers to make decisions about how to teach phonics and to clearly articulate these decisions to their colleagues and the community.

Reading and writing are more important than ever in a fast-moving technological world. Most children begin to read and write quite effortlessly in the first year of school, but some children face difficulties. In a recent report *Preventing Reading Difficulties in Young Children* (Snow, Burns and Griffin 1998), it was reported that children who are not at least modestly skilled as readers by the end of the third grade are unlikely to complete secondary school. Only a generation ago this did not matter so much, because the long-term economic effects of not becoming literate and completing secondary school were less severe. These days, excellent, high-quality instruction is essential in the early years of school where important foundations are laid.

Understanding phonics and the alphabetic principle can make learning to read and write easier to achieve, but if phonics instruction is inaccurate and confusing it can make this learning very difficult. An example of instruction that confuses children is a worksheet developed to practise segmenting and blending words to facilitate word recognition. The particular worksheet was designed with a key word *love* and the chunk 'ove' was alleged to have the same spelling–sound pattern in the other words. The other words listed on the sheet were *dove, above* and *glove.* But others listed – *Rover, stove* and *woven* – did not work. Worksheets like this confuse children's understanding of letters and sounds and can interfere with the clarity of early literacy instruction.

The importance of understanding the alphabetic principle – the idea that spoken language is made up of sounds that can be mapped to written letters – is shown in the following case study. The case study relates how a five-year-old boy, Fazal, learned about the alphabetic principle and also reveals the type of phonics instruction provided by his teacher.

Fazal: a case study

Fazal (not his real name) was about five years old and physically small but very strong when he began school in a school uniform that was large and would probably fit him for two years. He came to Australia from Ethiopia with his father, a political refugee, and two older sisters, and had been living with his elderly grandparents for quite a while although no-one knew how long. It is not clear what happened to his mother.

1 Fazal's classroom

Fazal found himself in a classroom learning English with 15 other children from different cultural and linguistic groups. Fazal and some of the other children were refugees and others were children of students completing post-graduate degrees. When he began school, Fazal refused to sit with the other children in a circle on the floor; he stood up, lay down, rolled over, and touched and sometimes annoyed the children near him with his heavy, new, leather pull-on boots.

After six weeks in school Fazal was writing and beginning to read. What did his teacher Chris Hastwell provide for Fazal in order for him to achieve these changes? There was no simple recipe for excellent instruction but, rather, a range of flexible teaching tools.

Chris decided that Fazal needed to move his body and use his hands and feet – in fact his whole body – as he explored the features of various objects and materials. Chris placed lots of play equipment in the classroom such as plastic animals, counters, shapes, objects to sort and classify, and Fazal was encouraged to play with these. He spent hours classifying according to left-to-right, right-to-left and then classifying according to color, shape, form and function. He explored one-to-one matching of objects in the sand-tray – for example, filling four plates with sand and giving each plate a knife and a fork.

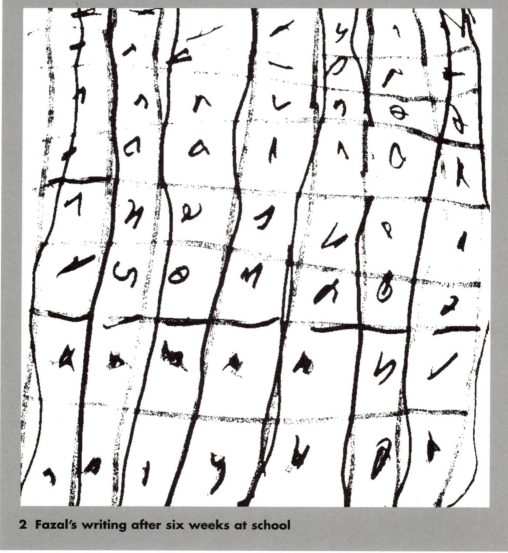

2 Fazal's writing after six weeks at school

An education worker who spoke one of the five Arabic languages Fazal could understand gave him 30 minutes of support for two days each week. Fazal was encouraged to write his name and experiment with paper and colored pens and he systematically studied written symbols and left-to-right directionality. He explored individual letters and created a grid structure for exploring directionality. After six weeks in school his writing looked like the example in figure 2.

What was Fazal learning here? According to the education worker the Arabic script, the written language he was most familiar with, is written from right to left and in the example in figure 2 Fazal is working out patterns of linear sequence, directionality and separating individual letter symbols.

3 An example of Arabic writing
'Welcome to our school'

In Arabic, letters are linked in groups and there is a range of symbols to depict the pronunciation of letters.

In English, individual and groups of letters represent particular sounds within spoken words. English is an alphabetic language, in contrast to the Japanese and Chinese written languages which are ideographic. Japanese has many graphemic symbols to represent syllables, and Chinese is morphosyllabic, using pictorial forms to create meaning.

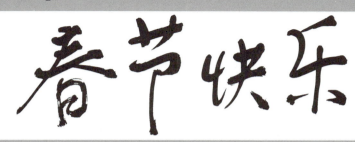

4 Chinese ideograph script in the classroom
'Happy New Year'

In the literacy activities in the classroom, Chris read books aloud. She involved the children in shared reading and writing for many different functions, and she had small groups of children in guided reading groups. Each day she organised activities for Fazal to cut out objects and letters from magazines. He first classified pictures of objects – plants, people, colors – and then he moved on to words and letters in all different kinds of fonts. He learned that the letter **h** can change size, color and font yet still remain the same letter.

5 Fazal's collage of the letter h

As the weeks continued, Fazal sometimes chose to join in with the other children in the classroom and he began to sit or lie on the floor when Chris read from a big book in shared reading. He watched the other children as they joined in on the chorus and repetitive syntax of the books. He looked avidly at the other children's faces, and copied their facial expressions and repeated the words and tone of the book being read together. After three months in school his writing showed great progress.

6 Fazal's writing after three months at school
'I like to play soccer and football.'

Fazal had grasped directionality, knew at least twelve letters and probably many more, and he knew that the letters represent sounds. At this time, he was reading emergent books where one word may change in a predictable sentence structure, for example 'I like apples. I like bananas.' He used the pictures to get to the meaning of the words and was beginning to attend to the print. His writing reveals that he knows that written English is made up of words, and that words have letters that represent sounds. He is possibly just beginning to understand that there are spaces between words but this is not demonstrated in his writing at this point.

The alphabetic principle of the written English language was grasped by Fazal early in his first year of school. This knowledge helped him to develop as a reader and writer.

A short glossary of terms

See page 75 for a more complete description of phonics terminology.

Phonics: the instructional practices that focus on the relationships between letters and sounds. Phonics emphasises how spellings of words are related to speech sounds in systematic ways.

Phonology: the way the sounds of the language operate.

Phonological awareness: the general ability to attend to the sounds of language as distinct from its meaning. It involves noticing phonemes, onset and rime, and syllables.

Phonemes: speech units that make a difference to meaning. The words *cup* and *pup* differ by one phoneme. Phonemes are usually written /s/. The word *pup* has three phonemes /p/, /u/ and /p/.

Phonemic awareness: the insight that every spoken word can be conceived as a sequence of phonemes.

Morphology: refers to the ways words are formed and relate to each other. The words *medic, medicine* and *paramedic* have a similar morphemic base that affects the spelling, even though the pronunciation may change.

Spelling: concerns the orthography or print whereas phonology relates to sounds. Spelling involves phonics as well as other strategies such as common letter sequences (eg 'com', as opposed to 'srk'), visual strategies (eg common patterns of words such as *light* and *night*), and morphemic strategies or how words represent meaning (eg *nation* and *nationality*).

CHAPTER ONE

The alphabetic principle
The al/pha/be/tic prin/ci/ple

> The methods by which we learn to read not only embody the conventions of our particular society regarding literacy – the channelling of information, the hierarchies of knowledge and power – they also determine and limit the ways in which our ability to read is put to use.
>
> Alberto Manguel, *A History of Reading* (1996: 67)

The alphabetic principle is the idea that letters in words usually stand for specific sounds. Readers and writers in the early stages of literacy learn the alphabetic principle – how sounds are represented in print.

The English alphabetic code is an amazing set of 26 letters that represent approximately 44 sounds or phonemes. It is an arbitrary, socially agreed upon set of conventions with a fascinating history. The set of symbols is organised to communicate meaning. Many languages, such as Chinese, use logographs (a form of picture) to represent meanings. Other languages can use symbols to represent whole syllables, whereas English uses letters to represent sounds in words. Because English has included words from many other languages there is not always a neat one-to-one correspondence between letters and sounds. For example, the words *eight* and *ate* sound the same but are written differently because they have a different meaning.

Even though English is not a regular phonetic language it is important to understand that there *is* a relationship between letters and sounds, and this is particularly important in beginning reading and writing. Many children understand the alphabetic principle – the relationship between letters and sounds – well before they recognise all the letters and sounds.

The alphabetic principle and writing

Children begin to think about sounds in words when they begin to write, and young children often use temporary spelling as they map sounds to letters. For example, when a child writes KAT for Kate they are giving 'A' a long /a/ sound like the name of the letter. When a child writes PPL for people they are using the names of letters to create a word.

Development of phonics in writing

When children begin writing they experiment with lines and pictures. As they develop they may move back and forth through several stages on the way to independent spelling. When teachers have to categorise children's writing for assessment purposes they are often looking for neat categories as a helpful organiser of information, but neat categories don't always fit all children.

The following examples show development in understanding letter and sound relationships – but these stages of writing are not always sequential.

PREPHONIC SPELLING

Children experiment with prephonic spelling when they use writing such as letters, numbers and other symbols to represent written language as they explore the relationships between written and spoken words. Sometimes a word is represented with a picture, and sometimes with letter-like symbols. There may be the beginnings of directionality from left to right.

7 Prephonic spelling
This child is experimenting with symbols and has copied a list of names from the classroom wall. In emergent literacy children are often fascinated by names. The child (aged 5) chose not to attempt unfamiliar words, preferring to copy lists instead.

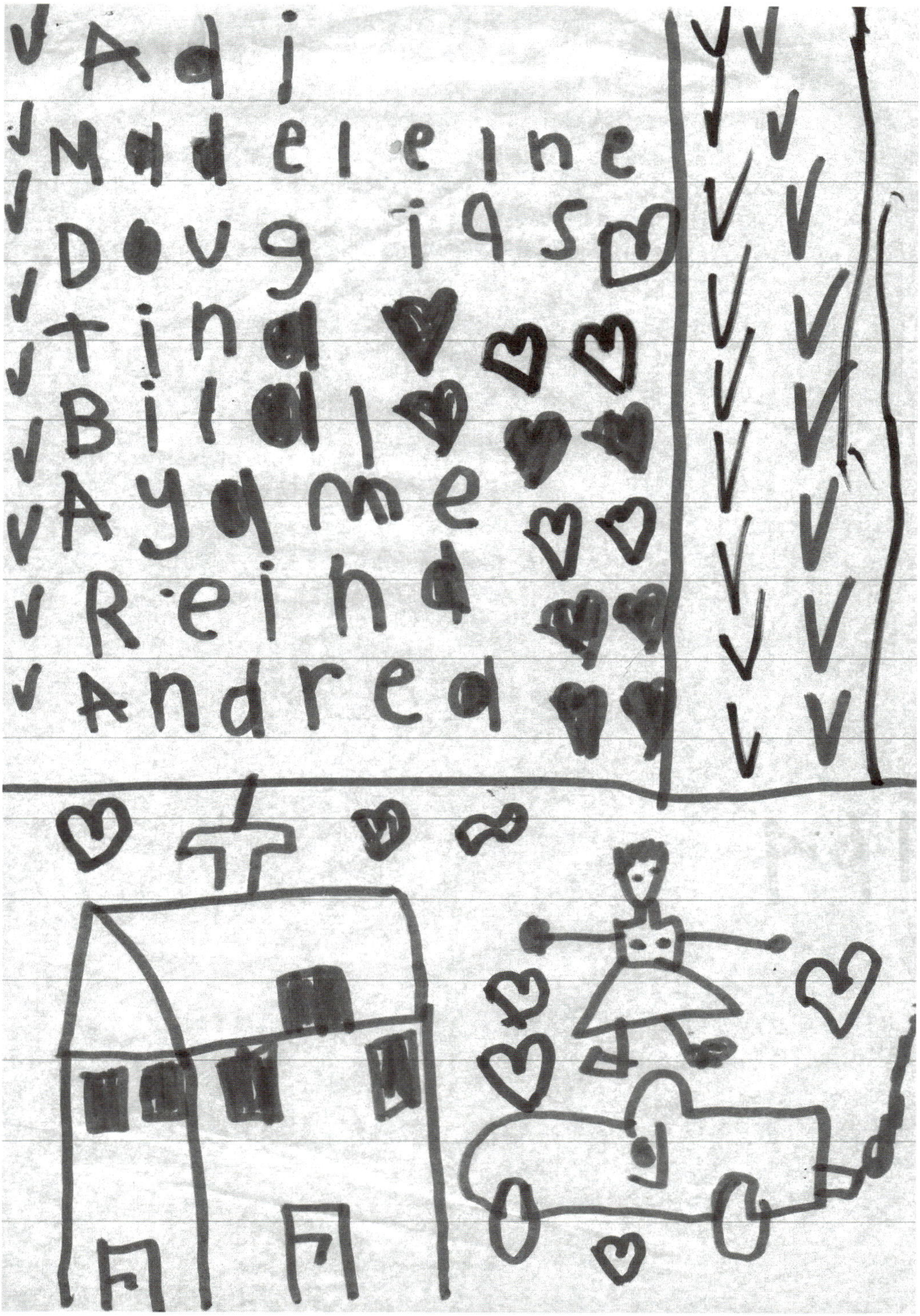
Adi
Madeleine
Doug 195
tina
Billal
Ayame
Reina
Andrea

SEMI-PHONETIC SPELLING

In semi-phonetic spelling there is a beginning understanding of sound–symbol relationships. A word may be represented with one letter or two. Usually the initial sound and occasionally a final sound is represented. Often letter names are used to represent sounds for example *lIk* for *like*. Often consonants are used and vowels are ignored, for example *skl* for *school*. Children may copy words from charts or books, as well as experimenting with writing letters by associating them with sounds.

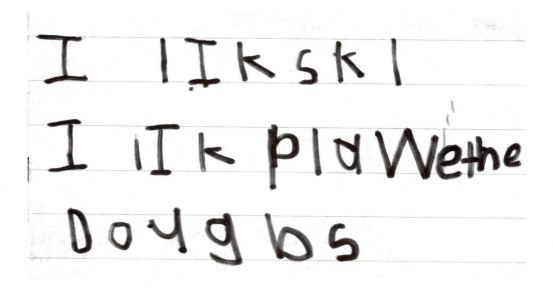

8 Semi-phonic spelling
'I like school. I like playing with Douglas.'

PHONETIC SPELLING

In phonetic spelling, writers record words using an almost perfect match of letters and sounds. Particular spelling of sounds can occur in a self-formulated style of spelling. The rules the writer invents may not conform to standard spelling, for example *wif* for *with*. There is also an increase in the use of words learnt by rote recall.

I Likeplaying FDBL and my brother got en his and my brother got othe beac

9 Phonetic spelling
'I like playing football and my brother goes to tennis and my brother goes to the beach.'

In figure 9 there are several conventional spellings, and many of these were copied from words displayed in the classroom. At this stage the child may not have a clear concept of word segmentation. The word *FDBL* for football is an example of semi-phonic spelling from the previous stage. The child is grappling with English syntax, and the use of repetitive sentences also points to a possible desire to practise what is known. Notice the style used for the letter *a* in *and,* which shows that the word has probably been copied from a book.

Satdie   nedad

10 Spelling examples
'Saturday, needed'

In figure 10, the words *Saturday* and *needed* were written phonetically according to the child's local dialect. This spelling shows a good knowledge of phonics and how it links to oral language. However, here it could be easy to fall into 'the phonics trap'. In the phonics trap, children with an accent that doesn't sound right to the monolingual ear of their teacher may be assumed to need more and more intensive systematic phonics. Yet this instruction may take time away from meaningful writing and reading. The phonics trap catches children and traps them in more and more phonics programs when it is not more phonics at all that is required as the child is using sound and letter relationships based on their own dialect. The phonics trap catches teachers too, locking them in to having too great a focus on narrow phonics instruction rather than more meaningful activities with texts.

TRANSITIONAL SPELLING

In transitional spelling, the writer begins to use a range of visual strategies such as common letter patterns. There is an increase in the use of words learnt by rote recall and a move away from relying on phonics for spelling all the words the child needs to write.

11 Transitional spelling

This example of transitional spelling shows a combination of spelling strategies which include words learnt visually (in this case *love*), words spelled phonetically, and complex spelling generalisations such as double consonants in words with inflectional endings such in the word *swimming*. Some words, such as the children's names, were copied from lists in the classroom.

INDEPENDENT SPELLING

In this phase, writers use a multiple strategy approach, at times using common letter patterns, phonics, and words learnt by sight. As spelling develops, more and more children rely on visual cues to decide whether the word looks right and whether there are other spelling alternatives.

> WHAT happened on the holidays
>
> On the holidays I went and saw Godzilla. I had a
> fanta and a jumbo icecream coated in chocolate at the movies,
> Me and Jessica Hill the Bruce Jim or Mum were the
> ony ones at the movies and Jessie had a coke and
> I slept right through Godzilla

12 Independent spelling

As children become more proficient at using visual cues they do not rely on phonics as a major strategy.

13 Children's writing
When children write they give a view of the strategies they are using.

The alphabetic principle and reading

The alphabetic principle is also important in reading, as the letters and sounds are one source of required information.

Readers need to use, and check against each other, four sources of information – visual, the letters, format and layout; phonology – the sounds and/or letters; the syntax or sentence structure; and semantics, illustrations or text meaning. Readers search for and use these multiple sources of information while reading as they search for the meaning of the author's message.

1. Visual information includes attention to the print and the letters in words. Attention to visual cues can be prompted by asking 'What have I noticed about this word?' 'Does the word look right?'
2. Phonology is the sound information that the reader uses from their oral language. Teachers often trigger attention to phonological cues by asking 'Does that word sound right to you?' 'Does that pattern of letters sound like this?'
3. The syntax or sentence structure is the cue the reader draws on from their experiences with oral language and from the book language of books read aloud. Teachers can focus the reader's attention on the syntax or sentence structure by asking questions such as 'Does it sound right if you say it that way?'
4. Semantics is the knowledge that coherent meaning can be constructed from a text. These meanings link to the reader's home and community experiences and also focus on the meaning that the author is communicating. Readers may ask questions about their reading such as 'Does this make sense?' 'Is this what the author is trying to say?'

Readers cross-check across these multiple cues to make meaning. A very skilful teacher has to decide what cue needs to be focused on in their teaching. For example, if a child reads:

✓   grub ✓ ✓ ✓ ✓

Text: The caterpillar is on a leaf.

the teacher might prompt the reader by saying 'Look at the first letter.' This is attention to the visual cue of letters.

If the child reads:

✓ leav ✓ ✓ ✓ ✓

Text: The leaf is on a tree

the teacher might draw attention to the sound and letter relationship in the word *leaf* by asking 'Is that last sound right?'

Sometimes the sentence structure or syntax may be a necessary cue in reading. For example if the child reads:

A ✓ ✓ ✓ ✓ ✓ ✓

Text: The leaves use sunlight to make food.

the teacher may prompt by asking 'Do those words sound right in the sentence?'

In the next example the meaning or semantic cues require attention.

✓ girl ✓ ✓ ✓ ✓

Text: The goat was by the gate.

The teacher may prompt the reader to search for meaning by saying 'Look at the picture. Is goat right?'

In all these examples the teacher prompted the reader to focus attention on the text. For example when the child miscues on the word *leaf* in 'The leaf is on a tree' the teacher does not draw on extraneous cues such as 'Look outside. Can you see a leaf in the sunlight?' This would shift attention away from solving the problem by exploring the text.

Readers use a range of strategies to create a match between the visual, structural, semantic and phonological cues. Readers who are making slow progress may often rely on using one cueing system above others – only using visual cues, for example. Some readers use semantics only, paying little attention to words and telling the story from the illustrations. Effective reading is learning to integrate multiple cues, and to cross-check, monitor by rereading and correct when necessary. The use of multiple cues is important for early reading, and many teachers explain to children that reading is problem solving, and that errors or miscues will occur as problems are solved.

The difficulty of texts also prompts a reader to integrate the cues in different ways. Sometimes an illustration or diagram will be of prime importance and sometimes decoding a particular word will be central.

Attending to print in reading

There are several features that signify growth as children move towards accurate word reading (Ehri 1995). These features show how children begin to attend more and more to print.

PRE-ALPHABETIC STAGE IN READING

In the pre-alphabetic stage, children decode words by using a visual cue such as two eyes in the word *look* for example. Instead of using the letters and sounds, they use the overall appearance of the word.

14 Using visual cues to decode

PHONETIC CUE READING

As children develop phonological awareness they begin to use partial sound information in the words, such as the initial or final sound. At this stage a child may substitute the word *goat* for *girl* when reading.

CIPHER OR FULL ALPHABETIC STAGE IN READING

At this stage, phonetic cue reading sometimes becomes less efficient as children analyse the words more deeply. Some readers become very labored, sounding out each letter in the word. This labored reading passes as the child is provided with more and more practice. In addition, the child learns to use a range of cues such as sentence structure and meaning, plus a body of automatically known high-frequency words, which makes reading more efficient.

15 Making and reading sentences

CHAPTER TWO

Phonological awareness

Pho/no/lo/gi/cal a/ware/ness

When children begin to read and write they require phonological awareness. Phonology and phonological awareness refer to the sound structure of speech and the way the sounds of the language operate and are produced. The phonological aspects of a language include intonation, stress and timing as well as attending to words, onset and rime, syllables and phonemes.

Phonology is a more inclusive term than phonemic awareness. Phonemic awareness is a specific term that focuses on small units of sound that affect meaning – the spoken word *dog* has three phonemes /d/, /o/ and/g/.

Phonological awareness of intonation, stress and timing occurs in rhymes such as *The Three Little Pigs* and in jingles, advertisements and songs on radio and TV. In *The Three Little Pigs* the refrain works because the emphasis placed on particular words and the timing for saying the refrain is very important.

> The wolf huffed,
> And he puffed,
> And he blew
> The house down.

In the refrain of three little pigs the individual words *huffed* and *puffed* sound the same except for the initial phonemes /h/ and /p/.

16 Listening to the sounds of language

Phonological awareness is the general ability to attend to the sounds of language as distinct from its meaning. Enjoying rhymes, noticing sound similarities (like *kite* and *light*)) and differences (*huffed* and *puffed*), and clapping the beat of syllables in words are indications of children's phonological awareness.

Phonological awareness can develop through word play with child-made rhymes like 'Hairy, beary, scarey' which captivate many young children. This captivation with sounds continues as children listen to and repeat jingles from television, nursery rhymes and pop songs. Children's awareness and fascination with sounds enables them to identify and play with rhyme, alliteration, words and sounds that are part of their spoken language.

Phonemic awareness

Phonemic awareness is not the ability to produce phonemes or the ability to discriminate between phonemes; rather, it is the awareness that phonemes exist as manipulable components of language. It is the conscious attention to the sounds in words.

For example, most babies make phoneme distinctions between speech sounds, and very early in life many can discriminate between *ba* and *pa* which have one phoneme that is different. Shortly after, they begin to practise the phonemes of their language, quickly moving on to the ability to produce them in speech.

As people develop they become so fluent with oral language that they learn not to attend to the individual phonemes, and this frees them up to concentrate on the higher order meanings and the nuances of language. We only need to go back and remember the phonemes if we begin learning to read another alphabetic script where 'we must learn to attend to that which we have learned not to attend to' (Adams 1990).

Phonemic awareness is more than discriminating between words and sounds. It is a conscious insight into the sounds in words.

> Phonemic awareness is the insight that every spoken word can be conceived as a sequence of phonemes. Because phonemes are the units of sound that are represented by the letters of an alphabet, an awareness of phonemes is the key to understanding the logic of the alphabetic principle and thus to the learnability of phonics and reading.
>
> (Snow, Burns & Griffin 1998: 52)

In many conventional phonics programs it was assumed that children had phonemic awareness. For example, a teacher might say: 'The letter **s** represents the sound /s/'. But if children don't have phonemic awareness they are unable to use this information about the letter **s** and the sound /s/. Phonemic awareness is necessary in order to take advantage of phonics instruction. However, once instruction in reading and writing begins, phonemic awareness and print knowledge increase. The more children read and write the more their knowledge of letters and sounds develops in an interactive process.

Phonemic awareness involves attention to words, syllables, rhyme, alliteration and analysis of phonemes.

WORDS

Phonemic awareness involves awareness of words and word spaces in oral language. When children speak, they do not usually concentrate on individual words. For example a child may say 'Wewenttothebeach'. When beginning to write the child may write:

Wewettthebech.

As children develop awareness of words and sounds they learn that words, in English, have spaces between them, and this awareness of words and spaces in spoken and written language is helpful for spelling, writing and reading.

SYLLABLES

Some words have one syllable or beat, such as *cat* and *Ann*, while others have two or more syllables, such as *can-dle* and *San-dy*. Becoming aware of the syllables in words helps children to write and read compound words like *birthday* and words with several syllables like *umbrella*.

birth day
um brel la

RHYME

When children become aware of rhyme they understand that it means words with the same final sound. Many children enjoy chanting raps and jingles and noticing the words that rhyme, and this is also the appeal of many Dr Seuss books. Research suggests that knowledge of nursery rhymes is related to the development of more abstract phonological skills and emergent reading abilities (Maclean, Bryant & Bradley 1987). However, raps, chants, advertising jingles and pop songs can be used in the same way to explore rhyme.

Are you hungry, my man.
Then we have a plan.
For dinner we do
The best that we can.

ALLITERATION

To develop awareness of alliteration the teacher may ask children to listen for the beginning sounds in words, saying, for example: 'What is the first sound you hear in these words?'

book, bed, baby, bottle
lovely licky lollipops

17 Language play with beginning sounds

ANALYSIS OF PHONEMES

Analysis of phonemes means the actual isolation of sounds in words. A teacher may explore children's understanding of phonemic awareness by saying words and asking children to listen for and identify the beginning, middle or final sounds. Analysis of phonemes is a complex activity and sometimes completion of the task relies on having a good memory rather than an ability to hear sounds.

Some teachers talk about stretching words to hear their sounds. For example see how the word 'week' is stretched so the sounds are easier to hear:

www eee kkk

When children begin to write and use invented spelling they learn to stretch out words to hear the sounds more clearly.

Hearing phonemes

The following tasks allow spoken words to be analysed for phonemes.

PHONEME SEGMENTATION TASKS

In phoneme segmentation tasks a child may be given a wooden stick and asked to tap out the number of phonemes heard in a one-syllable word. For example, given the word *mat*, the child should tap three times, once for each phoneme /m/, /a/, /t/.

A similar task was developed by the Russian psychologist Elkonin (1973) where the children were to lay out counters in boxes to represent each phoneme in a word spoken by the teacher.

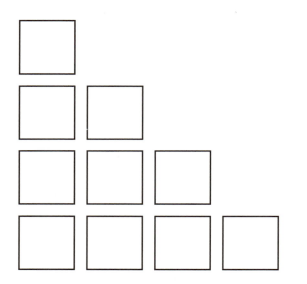

18 Elkonin boxes

For example the word *he* would have two counters for the two phonemes heard and the word *then* would have three counters.

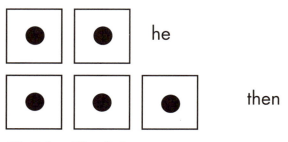

19 Using Elkonin boxes

Some children have problems with hearing phonemes in simple words like *he* because the phonemes run together. The Elkonin task generates a visual and discussible record of each child's effort to work out the sounds in words.

PHONEME MANIPULATION TASKS

In these tasks a child may be asked to say a word like *hill* without the /h/, saying 'ill'. They may be asked to say *monkey* without the /k/, making the word 'money', *nest* without the /s/ making 'net' or *pink* without the /k/, making 'pin'. These tasks require all manner of memory skills and mental gymnastics, and their place in enhancing early reading and writing is not clear.

monkey → money

hill → ill

SYLLABLE SPLITTING TASKS

Many educators claim that syllable splitting tasks are easier than phoneme segmentation tasks because children are asked to break off the first phoneme of a word or syllable. For example, a teacher asks the child to say the first sound in *pink* and the child says /p/. Next the child is asked to say what is left – *ink*.

This intersection between syllable splitting – c-at – and phoneme segmentation – /c/ /a/ /t/ – is where a current debate in phonics is taking place.

| c | at | onset and rime

/c/ /a/ /t/   individual phonemes

20 Syllable splitting (onset and rime) versus phonemic segmentation

Several teachers and researchers are asking the question about whether children can more easily analyse spoken words into phonemes or whether onsets and rimes are easier to manage. One argument is that onset and rime is a more natural way to make analogies from known words to unfamiliar words rather than sounding out phonemes (Moustafa 1997). (See page 30 for more on onsets and rimes.)

PHONEME BLENDING TASKS

In blending tasks the teacher provides the segments of a word, such as /m/, /a/, /p/ and the student has to put it together to make *map*.

Blending sounds to make words seems easier than phonemic segmentation and phoneme manipulation tasks. Researchers suggest that while phonemic deletion tasks such as 'leave out the first sound in hill' can only be completed as a result of early reading proficiency, phonemic blending may be an enabler in reading proficiency.

21 Using letters and sounds
Here a child uses letters and sounds to make written words.

PHONEME ODDITY TASKS

In phoneme oddity tasks, the child is presented with a set of three or four spoken words and asked which one is different or doesn't belong.

Sometimes the child is asked to listen for the first sound of the word to identify which is different:

sill pop pan pin

sometimes the last sound:

doll hop top

and sometimes the middle sound:

pin gun bun

These tasks require the child to compare and contrast similarities and differences and not break up words.

Levels of difficulty in phonemic awareness

There are several levels of difficulty in phonemic awareness tasks, and the following is a summary of the tasks in order of difficulty.

1 Knowledge of rhymes, jingles and chants and having an ear for the sounds in words.
2 Oddity tasks where children hear rhyme or alliteration of sounds. The child focuses on the components of sounds that make them the same or different.
3 Blending or syllable splitting where words are subdivided into sounds. In these tasks children must hear and produce sounds in isolation.
4 Phoneme segmentation tasks where words can be analysed into a series of phonemes.
5 Phoneme manipulation tasks where children can add delete or move any designated phoneme and generate a word from the result.

Levels 4 and 5 are generally unattainable by children who have not received formal reading instruction in preschool and school.

In early reading and writing the alphabetic principle is important. However neither phonemic awareness *alone* nor letter knowledge *alone* seems to be important in early reading. It is the linking or mapping of sounds to letters that is important.

Onsets and rimes

Many children find that dividing words into onsets and rimes is easier than splitting words into individual phonemes. For example, if a child is asked to listen to the word *dog* and then asked to say the sounds in the word, they may say d-og, which is using onset and rime rather than d-o-g which is the individual sounds.

The onset in a syllable is any consonant(s) that precedes the vowel. The rime consists of the vowel and any consonants that come after it. It is relatively easy to break the onset from the rime.

Word	Onset	Rime
I	—	I
itch	—	itch
sit	s-	-it
spit	sp-	-it
splint	spl-	-int
pie	p-	-ie
spy	sp-	-y

Children can use onsets and rimes to identify new words. For example, if a child meets an unfamiliar word *date* and knows the word *late*, they can use a process of analogy to work out the new word. Similarly, the known word *night* can be used to make a link to an unknown word *alight*.

It was <u>night</u> and the fire flies were <u>alight.</u>

Onset and rime is important because children use the concept to make analogies in both reading and writing. In fact 37 rimes make up nearly 500 words children use in early reading and writing (Adams 1990).

COMMON RIMES

-ack	-ail	-ain	-ake	-ale	-ame	-an
-ank	-ap	-ash	-at	-ate	-aw	-ay
-eat	-ell	-est	-ice	-ick	-ide	-ight
-ill	-in	-ine	-ing	-ink	-ip	-ir
-ock	-oke	-op	-ore	-or	-uck	-ug
-ump	-unk					

There are several advantages for using onset and rime in instruction for early reading:

- it is easier to distinguish initial onsets and rimes than individual phonemes
- children find rimes easier to identify than single final phonemes
- the awareness that different onsets can be spliced onto the same rime means that children can make different words
- more new words can be identified using onset and rime than the individual phoneme as the unit of analysis

Are letter names important?

An important predictor of beginning reading achievement is the ability to identify letters and a knowledge of the letter names. However, it is more complex than just teaching the letter names. It is the ease or fluency with which children can identify letters, and their familiarity with them, rather than just the accuracy in naming letters that is important.

A a B b C c

There are several explanations for the importance of knowing letters. A child who can confidently recognise most letters will have an easier time learning about letters, sounds and word spelling than a child who has to work at constantly remembering what letter is what.

Children who automatically see letters as wholes will quickly see that words are made up of patterns of letters. Children who do not easily recognise letters will often spend time working on identifying the individual letters. If children gloss over the uncertain letters, they may do so at the cost of needed growth in their visual vocabularies and, possibly, the correct meaning of a text.

In general, the names of letters are quite closely related to their sounds. There is evidence that a comfortable knowledge of the names of letters hastens children's learning of sounds because it mediates their ability to remember the sounds. If I, as a learner, know that this particular symbol is called **b** then I can use that fact to help myself remember that its sound is /b/.

Many children actually understand the alphabetic principle before they have mastered all the letters or been taught letter–sound correspondences. Knowing the letter names helps children remember their sounds, and the use of letter names helps children to induce the sounds. For example, when they are inventing spelling, children use letter names to spontaneously produce words such as KAN (can), AGRE (angry), BOT (boat), JRIV (drive).

The speed or automaticity in naming letters is related to reading achievement. Good and poor readers differ in the speed at which they can name letters.

What are phonic generalisations?

Phonic generalisations are rule statements such as 'e on the end of a word makes the vowel in the middle a long sound' or 'when two vowels go walking the first one does the talking'. Phonic generalisations are often useful for clarifying aspects of a particular word under study.

One problem with generalisations is that many rules only work fifty percent of the time. For example the rule 'e on the end of a word makes the vowel in the middle a long sound' works in *make, ripe* and *pane* but not in *have, give* or *done.* The rule 'when two vowels go walking the first one does the talking' works in *sheep, soap* and *rain* but not in *guess, could* or *blood.*

Phonic generalisations are useful teaching strategies to use when discussing unfamiliar words with children. However, they are not useful for designing worksheets with lists of words out of context and devoid of any meaning. Time spent reading connected texts and constructing connected writing is more valuable than isolating words by circling or coloring the same phonic generalisation.

Time spent reading connected texts is particularly important for children with reading problems. Unfortunately, repetitive worksheets tend to be given to children who learn differently, at a different pace or in a different way from other children. In fact children with reading problems were found to spend so much time on worksheets that they only read connected texts for about one minute per day, on average (see Stahl, Duffy-Hester & Stahl 1998: 342 for a discussion of this).

Phonological awareness and learning letter names is of huge benefit to young readers and writers. In fact letter knowledge is the single best predictor of first-year reading achievement and the ability to discriminate phonemes auditorily ranks a close second (Adams 1990).

CHAPTER THREE

Approaches to teaching phonics

Ap/proach/es to teach/ing pho/nics

Teachers are faced daily with many decisions about teaching phonics. They may be asked, 'In what order should the sounds of letters be introduced?' or 'Should consonants be introduced before vowels?' The answers to such questions depend on the students and the learning that is required. For example, a teacher may choose to teach the vowel letter 'A' and the sound /a/ because a child named Adam wants to write and read his name.

Questions about phonics teaching require thoughtful answers and this sections uses theoretical tools so that teachers can see where the particular phonics approaches are coming from. Using theoretical tools enables teachers to understand what the phonics approach values, and in turn enables teachers to make decisions about whether a particular approach fits their literacy program. Research studies show that teachers in practice tend to take what is useful from a range of approaches and use what will best orchestrate children's development in reading and writing.

The following questions about teaching phonics are based on the work of Adams (1990).
- Is it productive or destructive to pronounce letters in isolation?
- Should one teach the letter names or avoid using them altogether?
- In what order should the sounds of letters and spelling patterns be introduced?
- Should common consonants be introduced before vowels?
- Should vowels be introduced before consonants?

- Should the introduction of vowels and consonants be intermixed?
- Should short vowels be taught before long ones – or the other way around?
- For letters or spelling patterns that have more than one pronunciation, should alternative sounds be presented closely in time or considerably separated?
- Should letters that are visually easy to confuse be presented together to allow contrasts and comparisons or separated in time to minimise confusion?
- Should verbalisation rules (eg 'When two vowels go walking the first does the talking'; **g** can say /j/ only if it is followed by **e**, **i**, or **y**; every syllable in English must contain at least one vowel; a diphthong is two vowels together, both speaking, making a common sound') be emphasised or not?
- Is explicit training in blending productive or counterproductive?
- Should an initial reading vocabulary be selected on the basis of the frequency and familiarity of the words in the children's oral language or on the basis of frequency and regularity of the spelling patterns of the word?
- Should the children be thoroughly taught the letter-to-sound correspondences before words are presented?
- Should the literacy program begin with the presentation of some words before getting into phonics?
- Should meaningful, connected text be used from the start or saved until children have achieved some level of word reading?
- Should development of writing or spelling skills be initiated before, at the same time as, or after initial reading instruction?
- Should initial instruction be exclusively conducted with upper case letters or lower case letters?
- Are colors, diacritical marks, and modified alphabets helpful, harmful or neither?

Many of these questions are at the heart of the debates about teaching phonics, and there are arguments both for and against any simple answer. To move on from narrow debates about phonics pedagogy we need to take a wider lens and focus on literacy learners and what particular students need to learn next. Teachers can then adjust their teaching so that it works to improve the children's writing and spelling, and helps children to decode and comprehend texts with increasing ease.

This chapter discusses the many approaches to teaching phonics, and then uses theoretical tools to understand the views of teaching and learning that underlie the particular phonics approach.

The first three approaches to teaching phonics are traditional phonics approaches that have been used for many years and were very popular in the 1960s and 1970s. Aspects of these traditional approaches may still be apparent in current literacy programs; however, contemporary approaches to phonics teaching have more to offer most children who are learning to read and write.

Traditional phonics approaches

Synthetic phonics

Synthetic phonics approaches blend individual letters to make words. For example a teacher may write **s** on the blackboard and then say this letter **s** makes the sound /s/. Then the letters **u** and **n** are written and the children encouraged to blend the sounds to make the word **sun**.

s - u - n

Next, another word with an 'un' pattern is written and the children blend the word as the teacher points from left to right. Children practise phonics with worksheets.

Write and draw the words

s - u – n   f - u - n

- - -   - - -

r - u - n   b - u -n

- - -   - - -

I can run.   It is fun

In synthetic phonics, reading may consist of reading a decodable text with several 'un' words, 'I can run. It is fun.'

VAKT phonics (visual, auditory, kinaesthetic and tactile)

There are many different ways VAKT approaches are used. Most involve direct teaching of individual letters and sounds. The letters are traced while saying the name and sound, then letters are blended together to make words. One program which uses VAKT is the Spaulding approach (Spaulding & Spaulding 1962).

There have been many phonics programs that claim to accelerate literacy achievement by using motor skills and visual discrimination. In a review of research into learning with different modalities, such as tactile, kinaesthetic, visual and auditory procedures, Adams (1990) writes that there has been a tremendous amount of research on whether reading acquisition can be accelerated by training various nonlinguistic perceptual and motor skills such as spatial relations, visual memory, visual discrimination, visual motor integration, gross and fine motor coordination, tactile-kinaesthetic activities, auditory discrimination, and auditory-visual integration. However, despite the energy invested in such endeavors and despite the fact that many of the activities may be good for children in any number of ways, they seem not to produce any measurable pay-off in learning to read.

Analytic phonics

Analytic phonics begins with writing a word on the board that the child already knows such as *leg*. Next the teacher shows how the word can be broken into its component parts by saying something like 'The middle of the word *leg* has a short /e/ sound. The letter name is ee.'

Then a list of words with the short /e/ sound is written with the help of the children.

egg
wed

peg
shed

Often a worksheet on the short /e/ sound would be given out.

Circle letter e. Write and draw the words	
egg — — —	leg — — —
hen — — —	ten — — —
pen — — —	peg — — —

Using theoretical tools

Connectionism

Many traditional phonics programs draw on connectionist theory where priority is placed on cracking the code and decoding skills. In this view, elements or pieces are learned first of all then put together, or connected, to make a whole. This view stresses the benefits of over-learning letter forms, grapheme–phoneme associations and spelling patterns.

Connectionist theory emphasises reading automaticity which comes from over-learning. Children are expected to pass through a series of invariant stages on their way to literacy. Children who do not follow this progression, or who do not meet the specified objectives within a reasonable time are identified as needing remediation.

In connectionism:

- learning is based on the creation or strengthening of associations
- learning the alphabetic code and word recognition are the keys to successful literacy development
- direct, explicit teacher-led instruction is essential for beginning reading
- automaticity in decoding facilitates and precedes reading comprehension
- the act of reading can be broken down into isolated skills, which can be arranged into a hierarchy, taught directly, and then brought back to the whole (Crawford 1995)

In this view of literacy, decodable texts may be used. Decodable texts are often designed around narrow phonics rules, for example: 'The pig in this wig is big.'

Decodable texts may be helpful to some children who require decoding practice; however, many decodable texts can be criticised for not relating to the child's life and world, and not have much meaningful purpose for young children. Connectionist theory tends to focus on reading, with little concern about the process of writing, and does not stress the integration of listening, speaking, reading, writing and viewing.

Contemporary phonics approaches

Contemporary approaches to phonics include approaches where children make analogies between words they know and unfamiliar words. Many contemporary approaches are spelling based, and several focus on embedding phonics in meaningful text.

Analogy-based approaches

The idea in analogy-based approaches to phonics is that children who have never been taught by traditional phonics approaches learn to read by using predictable texts in language that is familiar to them and by making analogies between words they do know and unfamiliar words.

Key word

In this approach, children are taught to read and write 120 key words with common phonogram patterns and word parts. Five to six new words are introduced each week, with the teacher providing explicit instruction on how to use key words to decode other words (see Stahl, Duffy-Hester & Stahl 1998).

Guess the covered word

The teacher writes four or five sentences on the board and covers a particular repeated word in each sentence with sticky notes (Cunningham, Hall & Defee 1998).

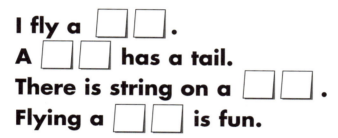

The word is covered before the vowel and then after the vowel. The children read each sentence and then make several guesses about the word. There are generally many possibilities for a word that will fit the context and the teacher points this out.

Next the teacher removes the sticky notes that cover the onset of the word, and children's guesses that don't have these letters are erased. Then new words that have the onset and fit the meaning are listed. When all the words that fit with the letters and the meaning are listed the entire word is revealed. It is suggested that teachers can adjust the length of the sticky notes so that children also become sensitive to word length.

Spelling approaches

There are many different spelling approaches to phonics where orthography, or the visual representation of words plus the phonemic features, are the key ideas. Three different spelling approaches – word study, making words and meta-phonics – are described by Stahl, Duffy-Hester & Stahl(1998).

Spelling approaches can be used to complement many existing literacy programs. Word study may occur as part of the writing program or in a reading lesson. Word study and word making activities can be undertaken by small groups in learning centres if master cards with instructions and answers, and packs of letters are made available by the teacher.

Word study

Children categorise words and word patterns by sorting words and pictures according to their common orthographical pattern. The orthographic features in words are then studied. For example, if a child is spelling 'rane' for 'rain' and makes other errors with a similar pattern, the teacher may begin instruction on long /a/ word patterns. In this approach, the teacher bases instruction on the words the children are writing but which they are confusing. This is teaching at the point of need, and in this approach children can usually see the purpose for spelling the word correctly.

Making words

This is an active, hands-on, manipulative activity in which children learn to look for patterns in words and learn how changing just one letter, or the letter order, changes the whole word (Cunningham & Cunningham 1992; Cunningham, Hall & Defee 1998).

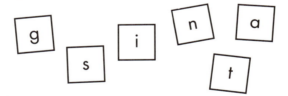

Children are given the six to eight letters that will form the final word. The lesson begins with making two-, three-, four- and five-letter words and continues until a word that can be formed with all the letters is made. At times the teacher calls out words with two, three, four and more letters that can be formed using the children's letters. At other times small groups work on making words. Children can sort the words using their common spelling patterns, beginning sounds, endings and rhymes or other orthographical features. The big word is related to something the children are reading.

For example, in one lesson the children had the letters **a**, **i**, **g**, **n**, **t**, and **s**, and they made these words:

it in an ant tan sit sat sag

snag sang gain stain giants

The word 'giants' was chosen as a word to focus on because the children had read a book about giants in a guided reading session. The last word made is the word that uses all the letters and this really captures the children's interests.

When all the words are made the teacher leads the children to sort them for onsets and rimes.

-it	-an	-ag	-ain
it	an	sag	gain
sit	tan	snag	stain

To conclude, the teacher leads children to make other words that have the same rime for example *hit, span, bag* and *brain*.

Meta-phonics

Meta-phonics is an approach where reading and spelling are taught simultaneously through social interaction and group problem solving (see Stahl, Duffy-Hester & Stahl 1998).

The key to the program is the articulation of sounds which are introduced in a phonemic awareness program. For example, the consonants /p/, /t/ and /k/ are introduced as popping sounds, and vowels are taught as glue letters. After learning several sounds and letters, children make consonant-vowel-consonant words – such as *cat, bin, cut* – and soon progress to more complex letter combinations such as *chat* and *thick*.

Using theoretical tools

Cognitive psychology

Several of the phonics and spelling programs previously described draw on cognitive and developmental psychology. In this perspective, children's literacy development centres on how young children chart and follow a cognitive course in determining how print and symbols work. The child is seen as an actor upon meaningful symbols within a literate environment. Children are active learners who build knowledge about conventionally accepted symbol usage. The teaching strategies stress cognitive processing with a focus on memory and conceptual associations.

Many cognitive psychology perspectives draw on developmental principles that reinforce the belief that generic patterns of literacy learning can be expected from all children. If there is a deviation from the series of cognitive developmental stages this may be seen as a problem or deficit.

In cognitive psychology:
- reading, writing and oral language are all integral parts of literacy learning
- literacy begins very early in life
- literacy learning happens best through active and meaningful engagement with written language
- children's literacy learning is characterised by a progression of developmental stages
- literacy education should be developmentally appropriate for children (based on Crawford 1995)

Integrated embedded approaches

In integrated embedded approaches to phonics instruction, the decisions about what phonics to teach arises from reading and writing connected texts.

Many teachers involve children in phonics in an embedded approach where meaningful reading and writing activities take place with texts developed around children's interests and needs.

Whole-to-parts phonics

In whole-to-parts phonics the words for phonic analysis come from the texts the children can read, or from texts read aloud by the teacher. For example, after a predictable text has been read aloud to the children, the teacher may ask them to select their favorite words in the story.

The teacher writes each word on separate cards, highlighting letters representing an onset (eg sm-) or a rime (eg -iles) and tells the children 'these letters say /sm/' and 'these letters say /ilz/'. The words are then placed on the classroom word wall (Moustafa, 1997). In time, as more and more words are placed on the word wall, they can be grouped into onset and rime patterns. For example words with a 'dr-' onset such as *drink*, *drip* and *drum* could be grouped together. The 'dr' blend can be highlighted with a pen to make recognition easier. At other times, the words may be organised in word families or rimes with all the '-ink', '-um' or '-ip' words grouped together. Onsets such as 'c-' that have at least two pronunciations, as in *cent* and *cat*, could also be grouped separately.

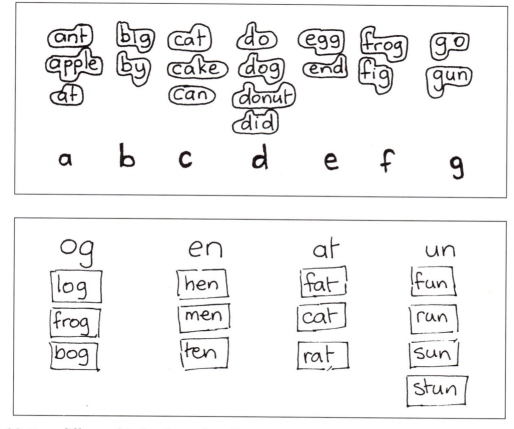

23 Two different kinds of word walls

Moustafa, in her book *Beyond Traditional Phonics* (1997), suggests that a flexible way of displaying words is to attach a plastic shower curtain to the classroom wall then, as the children choose the words and the teacher highlights parts of the words, the words can be attached to the plastic curtain with transparent tape. This allows for easy grouping and regrouping.

Whole-to-parts phonics is an analogy-based approach where children learn to decode words they do not know based on words or word parts they do know. For example, if a child can read *me* by comparing and contrasting word parts, the word *she* can be read. If a child can read *do* and *unhappy* the word *undo* can be read.

Whole-to-parts phonics is based on a theory of teaching reading where:
- children learn to read by reading
- early readers read better in the context of familiar language than outside of such contexts
- as children learn to recognise more and more print words in the context of familiar language they use their knowledge of words they already recognise to pronounce words they don't recognise
- the more children read, the more proficient they become (Moustafa 1997)

Whole-to-parts phonics claims that, contrary to many traditional beliefs about learning the alphabetic principle, children have difficulty analysing spoken words into phonemes when there is more than one phoneme in an onset or a rime. Whole-to-parts phonics is different from traditional phonics in several ways.

Traditional phonics	Whole-to-parts phonics
systematic, explicit, extensive	systematic, explicit, extensive
based on assumptions dating back to Socrates	based on recent discoveries in linguistics and psychology
goes from parts to whole (from letters to words)	goes from whole to parts (from whole text, to words, to word parts)
instruction occurs before reading	instruction occurs after reading (eg after a predictable story is read *to*, *with* and *by* children.
teaches letter-phoneme correspondences	teaches letter-psychological parts of speech correspondences (in English, letter-onset and letter-rime correspondences; in Spanish, letter syllable correspondences)
teaches inconsistent rules	teaches multiple possibilities
abstract, difficult to remember	contextualised, memorable
logical, makes sense to literate adults	psychological, makes sense to children learning to read

24 Traditional and whole-to-parts phonics (based on Moustafa 1997: 92)

The whole-to-parts instructional approach seems to rely on children having some knowledge of initial letters and phonemes. The more written words children recognise, the better position they are in to make analogies between familiar words and unfamiliar words.

Embedded phonics

Embedded phonics takes place when sound–letter relationships are explored in the texts the children have already read. Reading Recovery makes use of an embedded phonics approach.

Reading Recovery is a one-on-one tutoring program designed for children in the lowest 20% of first grade. The lessons have a common structure. First, the child selects and reads one or two books that are at their independent reading level. Next, the teacher reintroduces a book at the child's instructional or learning level. This text would have been introduced on the previous day. This instructional text should present some challenges to the child but there should be enough familiar words for the child to read at 90–95% accuracy. When the teacher introduces the book, they talk through the text introducing, through conversation or talk about the book, new vocabulary and sentence structures. The teacher may read aloud part of the book as an introduction but vocabulary is not pre-taught before reading.

The idea is that children learn to problem solve by cross-checking using several information sources. The information sources in Reading Recovery are meaning or semantics, sentence structure or syntax, sound and letter relationships, and visual which includes the letters, layout and format of the text. These multiple information sources are used by readers as they monitor their reading behavior and self-correct if errors are detected.

After the particular book has been introduced, the child reads it as the teacher observes the child's problem-solving strategies. Based on observations of the child's reading behaviors the teacher may introduce one or two teaching points following the reading.

A teaching point in Reading Recovery may be to focus on integrating several information sources in reading; however, a common teaching practice is making and breaking words using magnetic letters. This is an analogy-based approach to phonics where words from the text just read are made up with plastic letters and then broken down to make new words for example:

m ake

b ake

c ake

After the making and breaking activities the child writes a sentence-length story with the help of the teacher. The sentence is then cut up into individual words and reassembled. There may be some additional work with Elkonin boxes where the child is asked to place counters in boxes corresponding to the sounds heard in particular words. To conclude the lesson a new, carefully levelled text is introduced and the child attempts to read it. This new book is reread at the next session.

The phonics instruction in Reading Recovery takes place after reading and writing connected texts. The phonics component is relatively small compared with the amount of time spent reading books and writing.

Guided reading

In classrooms where small group instruction in guided reading (Fountas & Pinnell 1996; Hill 1999) takes place, the making and breaking of words and attention to sounds and letters can occur in the small guided reading groups. Attention to sounds and letters takes place after the book has been introduced and the children have read it. The focus or target words for study and analysis are selected from the book that has been read so that the words are first met and read in context.

Children also have an opportunity to engage in further word study in literacy learning centres which can be organised to free the teacher to work with one guided reading group. These can include a writing centre, a word-making centre, a book-browsing centre, a buddy-reading centre, a word-game centre, and more. Again, the focus is on learning about sound and letter relationships that occur in the books the children have read.

Using theoretical tools

Social constructivism

Many embedded approaches to phonics draw on social constructivist theories. In this view, literacy development takes place with social support in interaction with others and involves the development of skills with culturally developed tools that mediate intellectual activity (Vygotsky 1978; Rogoff 1990). In a Vygotskian-based early literacy curriculum, literacy is a cultural tool which acts to transform behavior as this behavior is internalised.

Social constructivists claim that children are competent and capable users of oral and written language and that formal literacy education should build on these competencies. Children purposefully learn and make sense of the complex semiotic signs and symbols of their culture. This meaning-making – or sense-making – process in the young child is no different from the processes engaged in by older children and adults.

In a social constructivist perspective, reading and writing activities of even very young children reflect their culture and are characterised by both purposefulness and intention. The differences between the processes of young readers and more proficient language users is a matter of sophistication, practice and experience, not just a particular stage of psychological development.

In social constructivism:
- language and literacy are socially constructed
- language and literacy are culturally specific
- there is no one set of universal, invariant developmental stages
- literacy is based on the intent to make sense of social events
- young readers and writers engage in the same types of literacy processes, though at a less sophisticated level, as those engaged in by older children and adults (based on Crawford 1995)

25 Children engaged in a readers theatre performance of the text

More theoretical tools

The theoretical tools of connectionism, cognitive psychology, and social constructivism enable teachers to see the underlying assumptions of different phonics approaches. In the discussion of phonics a further theoretical tool, poststructuralism, is needed. Poststructuralism encourages a focus of the child's sociocultural identity which has to do with gender, race, social class and the power relationships within these.

Poststucturalism

In poststructural views, literacy development is related to culturally valued literacy events and human identity. Children begin to construct and reconstruct their identities well before formal school. They learn how to conduct themselves in complex social events with different rules for participating in conversations. These events are tied up intimately with the learning of community values, ideologies and 'namings' of the social and natural world. They are also a means for establishing identity and playing out age, gender and authority relations with caregivers (Luke 1993). If a home-based primary discourse, the language spoken at home, is similar to the secondary discourse of school this can facilitate learning, but as Gee (1987: 9) notes:

> Children from non-mainstream homes often do not get the opportunities to acquire dominant secondary discourses including those concerned with the school in their homes, due to their parents' lack of access to these discourses. At school they cannot practice what they haven't yet got and they are exposed mostly to a process of learning and not acquisition. Therefore, little acquisition goes on.

This is important for understanding children's use of invented spelling, particularly in early writing, as many children may use different syntactic patterns and pronunciation from the teacher. This also explains why some children do not choose to use invented spelling and feel more comfortable copying words correctly.

In a poststructural view there is a close relationship between language and identity. It is through language and interactions with others that people construct themselves. Individuality is a product of nature and biology, and 'subjectivity' is the product of social relations. Subjectivity is a social construction and each one of us has a matrix of 'subject-positions' that may be inconsistent and contradict each other.

This matrix of positions explains why a person with strong feminist views will behave differently at work, at home and with friends. Similarly, this helps to explain why a boy in a small group engaged in a particular phonics task may respond differently in the school group, the play ground and at home. There is not one unique subjectivity but many fluid subjectivities that vary across and within different social interactions.

How people think of themselves and their world – their sociocultural identity – signals membership of a particular group. Race, social class and gender are dynamic aspects of the sociocultural identity kit and interact in a multiplicity of ways to make meaning.

Learning about phonics does relate to people's identity. For example, in a school in a remote desert community a group of children used worksheets about 'Eskimos' and icicles to identify and practise the letters **e** and **i**. Attention to the local culture may have led to totally different tasks that were more responsive to the knowledge and experiences of the children. Similarly, the texts used, particularly in the early stages of reading and writing, must reflect the life experiences of the children.

In poststructuralism:

- language and literacy learning is facilitated when there is a close match between home and school discourses
- issues of gender, social class and race are embedded in literacy
- power relationships in school relate to gender, social class, race and relationships between children and teachers (Solsken 1993; Shannon 1990)

If teachers see children as made up of many subjectivities and in the process of continually reconstructing and being reconstructed by others, then careful attention to the classroom dynamics, learning activities, the texts and the forms of talk that goes on in the classroom is fundamental.

Using theoretical tools to help make decisions

Using theoretical tools helps teachers to make decisions about what approach to take when teaching phonics. From a connectionist point of view, beginning literacy usually has a focus on cracking the code. Cognitive psychology provides insight on how multiple cues and strategies are used to teach phonics. Social constructivism stresses active apprenticeship models of learning with meaningful texts that relate to the children's social and cultural worlds. Poststructuralism provides a focus on identity, meaning and the way power is at work between teacher and student and between student and student in small groups, and in individual and whole-group instruction.

In the busy classroom, many teachers use a combination of approaches to teaching phonics and they draw on a range of ideas and activities. A recent study revealed that teachers – whether labelled 'whole-language' teachers or 'skills-based' teachers – find the notion that phonics not being taught in whole-language classrooms is inaccurate (Baumann et al 1998). Teachers generally do not assume a polar 'either or' approach to phonics and whole language, but instead provide children with a balanced, eclectic program involving both reading skill instruction and immersion in rich literacy experiences. Many teachers see the debates about phonics versus whole language as one that diverts attention, energy and resources from the real challenges teachers face trying to understand what children know and what they need to learn next.

Questions about teaching phonics

Some questions about teaching phonics remain. Is phonemic awareness really the key to identifying sounds for writing and reading? Should phonics be taught as early as possible at home and at preschool? Is environmental print important in early literacy? How does invented spelling relate to phonemic awareness? Should phonemic awareness training programs be developed as early as possible?

Is phonemic awareness the key to early literacy?

There is little doubt that phonemic awareness has a relationship with success in beginning reading, but decontextualised phonemic awareness training programs are not the answer for most children.

How early can phonics be taught?

Successful methods of reading instruction have been developed with children at three and four years of age. The bottom line is that the role of chronological age is not one of limiting what a child can learn but of limiting the ways in which they can effectively be taught. Attention to phonological awareness has traditionally been important in the preschool years. It is how the sounds of language are taught that is critical.

What role does environmental print play in learning to read?

In the field of emergent literacy, reading environmental print has been noted as an important beginning. Children read Coca-Cola and McDonald's logos and signs.

The reading that occurs at this stage is known as logographic (Goswami 1994). The processing of logographic symbols is not that of processing alphabet letters in the print. However, reading and gaining meaning from signs and symbols is the beginning of making sense of written texts.

Are training programs in phonemic awareness effective?

There are two main ways of developing phonemic awareness. One is learning to hear sounds in connected language; the other is phonemic awareness training programs.

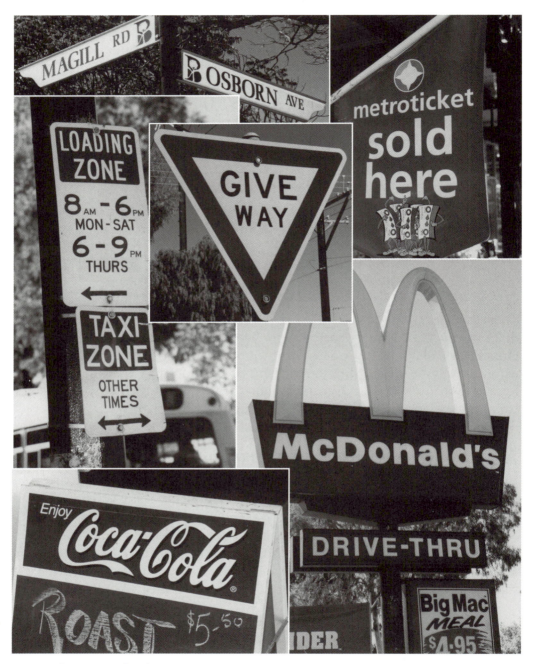

26 Environmental print
Reading environmental print has been noted as an important beginning to emergent literacy.

In narrow training programs there is often a series of exercises where children identify similar or different sounds in spoken words. One can question the meaningfulness and relevance of such training programs and ask how they relate to learning to read and write. For example, what happens to a child who is included in a phonemic awareness training program and who has no clue that words exist in print or that written language says something meaningful? How do children interpret and make sense of that training? For example, if a training program has narrow phoneme oddity tasks, where the child is presented with a set of three of four spoken words and asked which one is different or doesn't belong (eg *sill, pop, pan, pin*), how does this link to early writing and reading?

The research is not clear on the benefits of narrow approaches to teaching phonemic awareness. We need to explore whether children who develop phonemic awareness over time, as they interact in meaningful literacy events, have a different way of operating with phonemic awareness than do children who have been in narrow, decontextualised phonemic awareness training programs. It is quite possible that narrow phonemic awareness training programs only advantage those students who already have a larger picture of the purpose and functions of spoken and written language.

How does invented spelling relate to phonemic awareness?

An inventive speller's playing with sounds and letters when writing helps to consolidate phoneme awareness. The process of invented spelling is essentially a process of developing phonemic awareness.

The evidence that invented spelling activity simultaneously develops phonemic awareness and promotes understanding of the alphabetic principle is extremely promising. Developing phonemic awareness through invented spelling is an important idea especially in view of the difficulty with which children are found to acquire these insights through other methods of teaching (McGee & Purcell-Gates 1997; Richgels 1995).

In fact invented spelling performance may predict reading achievement as much as a year later, as measured in various ways (in word identification measures, and reading comprehension measures).

The importance of making connections

The fact remains that even in carefully planned instructional programs children take up different knowledge and skills. Even the best planned lesson will be received differently by different children.

If a teacher embeds phonics in meaningful contexts, and models and demonstrates how phonics works then one single teaching event can work on multiple levels. One child may learn a phonic generalisation, another may problem solve using various cues and another will solve problems they have been on the verge of solving.

The understandings about phonological awareness are best taught when they are embedded and connected with the other processes operating in concert. It is this rich interconnected, embedded knowledge that supports literacy learning. Many children play with phonemic awareness in songs, TV jingles, chants and nursery rhymes and it is the skill of effective teaching that makes this knowledge clear and obvious to children.

But there are always exceptions to the rule. What happens to children who are involved in programs with lots of literature, songs and functional literacy events yet who cannot perceive language at the phoneme level? Do some children come to school aware of the many functions and forms of written language and yet not, for a range of factors, develop phonemic awareness through these activities?

There is no one path to becoming literate; rather, there are multiple paths. Despite this, there is evidence of the need to embed emergent literacy in functional purposes. It is the ways in which teachers help children to make connections between the different aspects of literacy that is important.

These connections are best made as literacy is woven in and through the fabric of classroom life, the school culture, peer culture activities and the community.

CHAPTER FOUR

Practical phonics ideas
Prac/ti/cal pho/nics i/deas

Phonics teaching can take place using everyday print in the community. Teachers can use a label from a can of soup, a retail catalogue, or words from a song or jingle – and a phonics lesson pops out.

Using everyday print

How can everyday print on street signs and advertising boards be used to teach phonics? In the following example the teacher engages in teaching sound–letter relationships in everyday, functional literacy activities.

To begin the lesson the teacher wrote out, on a chart, a poem called 'Chicken Soup with Rice' by Maurice Sendak. This poem is about outdoor winter play on ice and eating chicken soup with rice. On a chair next to the chart the teacher placed a large institutional-sized can of Campbell's chicken soup with rice.

26 Using everyday print to teach phonics

After discussing then reading the poem, the teacher asked the five-year-old children to guess what she had brought in from the grocery store. The chicken soup was to be part of a cooking activity later in the week, and now it was the context for making connections between poem print and label print. The teacher's questions prompted children to notice letters, words and sounds and these were interwoven with discussions of the meanings and functions of written language.

Mrs P: I brought in something today I wanted to show you. I was at the supermarket last night ... and I was looking at the soups. And I saw all sorts of soups. I saw vegetable soup, and I saw tomato soup, and I saw broccoli soup, and I saw cheese soup –

Child: Cheese soup?

Mrs P: – and I saw onion soup, and I saw this soup!

Child: What is it?

Child: I know what it is. Chicken soup.

Mrs P: Do you think so?

Child: Chicken noodle soup.

Child: No.

Child: Yeah! I can read it.

Child: Chicken soup.

Child: Chicken noodle soup.

Child: *Chicken* starts with a *T*.

Child: My favorite food is chicken noodle soup.

Child: My favorite one, my favorite soup is chicken noodle!

Mrs P: Is it your favorite kind?

Child: Me too. We're just like each other!

Mrs P: You agree with each other ... There are lots and lots of words on this can of soup. Is there a word up here that you think you can read? On the can?

Children: *Chicken, Chicken* ...

Mrs P: Where do you think it says *chicken*?

There was some discussion about the brand name Campbell's and a boy in the class named Campbell. Then the conversation went back to reading the label.

Mrs P:	Why do you think that says *chicken?*
Child:	Chi- Chi's Chi-chi [pronounced Chee-cheez, chee-chee]
Teacher:	What do you think, Kait?
Child:	Chuh ...
Mrs P:	You're thinking. You know, Erin, you're right. That is the word that says *chicken*. Right there. If you look at the *chicken* word in the poem ... See the *chicken* word here in the poem? [points to and reads a line that includes the words *chicken soup with rice*] There's the *chicken* word right there. Can you find the *soup* word?

(Transcript based on Richgels, Poremba & McGee 1996: 639)

This transcript shows how letters and sounds can be introduced in a manner that preserves children's initiative and problem-solving strategies. Children are keen to investigate sounds and letters, but the teacher has to listen carefully to what children are finding and adjust her responses accordingly. In this process, there is explicit teaching of sounds and letters and of the literacy strategies of word matching, and use of syntactic and semantic cues, as well as reading different texts for different purposes. Further analysis of sounds and letters could take place as children make a list of *ch* words, or make words that rhyme with *rice*.

In this contextualised approach, the children are made consciously aware of their cognitive processing in reading. They also learn to learn effective strategies from others in the classroom. This approach to teaching phonics in meaningful context contrasts sharply with approaches where phonic generalisations are taught in an isolated fashion.

Some children require many examples of how phonics works in meaningful events such as reading information on signs and labels. Some children don't see the purpose of learning letter and sound relationships unless they are shown how they work in reading and writing. Some children have difficulties learning the correspondence between sounds and letters, and many children who experience difficulties in reading have trouble transferring the phoneme-to-letter correspondences acquired in spelling to the letter-to-phoneme correspondence in reading. Many children require activities in which they isolate the sounds in words and make, break and build new words with plastic or cardboard letters.

Using books

Children can explore sounds and letters in books that are read aloud. For example, Dr Seuss books, which are based on rhyme and word play, are greatly enjoyed by most children. Catalogues, magazines and leaflets can be use to cut out print and make collages to help children to recognise and name the letters of the alphabet.

Another way of introducing sounds and letters is known as 'rounding up the rhymes' (Cunningham, Hall & Defee 1998). This occurs after reading a big book or a small book aloud many times. For example, after several readings of the book *Ten Little Dinosaurs* (Schnetzler 1996) which describes the actions of 10 different dinosaurs, the teacher draws the children's attention to the rhyming words.

> Five little dinosaurs playing in the street
> Ankylosaurus yelled, 'A car to beat!'
> He charged into the street:
> squeal, screech, bleet, spleet.
> No more dinotanks playing in the street.

As children notice the rhyming words – some of which are nonsense words – they are written on index cards and put in a pocket chart (strips of plastic attached to a board to make 'pockets'). The following words were 'rounded up' from several pages.

bed	bike	mooth	river	peak	street
head	spike	tooth	aquiver	beak	beat
said	trike	booth	shiver	shriek	speet

Next, because the focus was the words that have the same spelling pattern and same sound, some words are deleted. Then five sets of words that rhyme and have the same spelling pattern are left in the pocket chart.

bike	mooth	river	peak	street
spike	tooth	aquiver	beak	spleet
trike	booth	shiver		

The next stage is critical, as it is the transfer stage where children use analogy based on spelling patterns to create new words. Some new words created to fit the spelling pattern and rhyme were:

hike   liver   leak   sweet

Using jingles, raps and rhymes

Poems, songs, jingles, raps and rhymes are ways to draw children's attention to the sounds of language. If the jingles and rhymes are written on large charts, children can explore the connection between sounds and the visual letters. When focusing on spoken language the children's attention is drawn to the phonemes or sounds.

JINGLES

Jingles are word play that uses repeated sounds and rhymes, and are usually about nonsense topics. Jingles which focus on rhyme and rhythm can be generated by children and the teacher and written on large sheets of paper.

A	H	X
Ants in your pants	A happy hippopotamus	Extra exciting
Ants in your pants	Has hopped into my bed.	Extra cool
Smack and whack them	He thinks that he is hiding,	Extra excellent
Smack and whack them	But I can see his head.	Xs rule.
Ants in your pants	Hip-hip-hip-potamus!	
	Hip-hip-hip-hooray!	
	Who's that hippopotamus?	
	Who knows?	
	He didn't say.	

ALPHABET RAPS

The names of children in the class are combined with rhyming words to make a rap to chant, read and perform. Names can have one, two or three or more syllables and the rhyming words may have to be changed to fit the rhythm. The rap can also be changed to fit better with different words used in different social communities.

> A is for Adam, apple and Ann,
> B is for Barry, berry and ban.
> C is for Connie cabbage and cog,
> D is for David, dinner and dog,
> E is for Erin, egg and excite,
> F is for Fay, fish and fight.

SONGS

Many well-known songs can be adapted to play with sounds. For example the song 'Old MacDonald Had a Farm' can be sung with a focus on initial sounds, medial sounds or end sounds (Yopp 1992).

> What's the sound that starts these words
> *Yellow, yes* and *yet?*

[Wait for a response from children.]

> /y/ is the sound that starts these words:
> *Yellow, yes* and *yet?*
> With a /y/, /y/ here and a /y/, /y/ there,
> Here a /y/, there a /y/, everywhere a /y/, /y/.
> /y/ is the sound that starts these words:
> *Yellow, yes* and *yet.*

and so on.

   In another example, initial sounds can be substituted in 'I Have a Song That We Can Sing' (which is sung to the tune of 'Someone's in the Kitchen with Dinah').

> I have a song that we can sing.
> I have a song that we can sing.
> I have a song that we can sing.
> It goes something like this:

Fe-Fi-Fiddley-i-o
Fe-Fi-Fiddley-i-o-o-o-o
Fe-Fi-Fiddley-i-ooooo
Now try it with the /z/ sound!

Ze-Zi-Ziddley-i-o
Ze-Zi-Ziddley-i-o-o-o-o
Ze-Zi-Ziddley-i-ooooo
Now try it with the /y/ sound!

and so on.

The same kinds of substitutions can be made to the Ee-igh, ee-igh, oh! sections of 'Old MacDonald Had a Farm'.

Levels of phonemic awareness

There are at least five different levels of phonemic awareness that can be used with jingles, raps and songs.

WORD AWARENESS

This involves breaking spoken language, nursery rhymes, chants and songs into words. In a simple sentence 'This is a cat' the child can hear four separate words.

SYLLABLES

Words such as the names of people and things can be broken into syllables, or beats, and clapped or snapped with the fingers: Su-san, Im-ran, Fay.

RHYME

The child hears a rhyme and can produce a word that ends with the same sound.

ALLITERATION

Alliteration, which is hearing words that begin with the same sound, is a beginning sound analysis skill.

ANALYSIS

In oddity tasks, where the children hear what's the same and what's different, they listen for alliteration or rhyme. The sounds can be in the initial, medial or final position and new words can be invented and added to songs and jingles. Here the child focuses on and hears the components of sounds that make them the same or different.

BLENDING

This is where parts of words or syllables are given and the child blends the parts together to produce a word. The words can be subdivided into syllables or sounds, involving onset and rime such as *c-at, m-at, ch-at*, syllables such as *ca-ter-pil-lar*, or individual phonemes such as *h-o-t*.

MANIPULATION

In manipulation tasks children add, delete or move a sound and generate a word from the result. For example, the child hears the word *cat* and can delete and add a sound to make the new word *rat*.

Children's names: a way to begin

Many teachers use children's names as an engaging starting point for exploring the relationship between sounds and letters. Names such as Oscar, Max, Yoko and Maria are important to children's identity. Parents give their children a name which reflects gender, culture, religion, history, family names and the parents' hopes for their child's future.

The names given for people and objects, in general, are also important for learning. Giving names to other people and objects is a way for young children to classify and order sensory experiences. Names and symbols allow people to talk about absent objects and share communication with others.

Learning that things have arbitrary labels or names given to them by people is an important social and cognitive milestone. Naming allows children to find relationships between things and to talk about similarities and differences.

Ways to work with names

Make two sets of cards with children's names. These can be classified into names that begin the same way, names that have the same sound, names that end alike, and so on. Matching games such as Snap and Concentration can be played with the cards.

- Write names on paintings and personal belongings.
- Write children's names on card covered with plastic they can trace, and use the card as a writing model.
- Paint names with water outside on the playground.
- Make a 'Who am I?' book where children write clues to their identity and other children guess their name.
- Use children's names such as 'Stephen will you …'and encourage children to use each other's names whenever possible.
- Make a class photograph album with photographs and children's names.
- Make a class book with photographs and a short description of each child in the class.
- Make a school-wide teachers' book with photographs and a story about each teacher.
- Make a mural of the class and add names.
- Explore the meaning of children's first names.
- Explore names that are similar in the community.
- Explore the meaning of last names for example, Smith, Barber, Tailor.
- Trace the history and geographical location of the children's last names.
- Place last names on a map of the world to show where names may have come from.
- Use lists of names on birthday calendars.
- Write names of group members and lists of who goes to the library or has special roles to play in the classroom.
- Explore patterns in children's names by clapping the beat in the name; Jen-ny, Ti-mo-thy, Ste-pha-nie. Children can use musical instruments to create the beat, or dance, hop or jump to the beat.
- Make name alliterations into a class book. Use names and a verb such as Sue sews, Jim jumps, Alex amazes. Names can also be combined with positive adjectives, excellent Emma, brilliant Bob, sensible Steve, lively Liz, kind Kate, soft Sara, elegant Eleanor and jolly John.
- Read poems about names such as A. A. Milne's 'James, James, Morrison, Morrison' and Eve Merriman's poem 'Spring Fever' which has alliteration of names such as Frank frets, John jumps.

- Have a name change day when a sound such as /b/ is used at the beginning of each name, for example David becomes Bavid, Susan becomes Busan and so on.
- Change the characters in stories read aloud to the names of children in the class.
- Make a class address book using children's names.
- Make a class birthday book with children's names.
- Make lists of names and classify them into friends' names, pets' names, football team names, sports star names, teddy bear names and so on.

Introducing sounds and letters

What letter sequence to teach?

There is no particular sequence for introducing sounds and letters. However, most teachers begin with the most easily identified letters like **s.** They may teach a sequence of consonants which have distinct characteristics, for example **s, m, f, n, t, w, h** and then the vowels **a, e, i, o, u.** This combination of consonants and vowels enables children to build words that begin with the same sound:

sun   sat   sit

Teachers can also support children to use word family analogy with onsets and rimes such as:

cat   mat   fat   sat

The easily confused sounds, for example m/n, p/b, f/v, s/z and r/w, should be introduced separately. Letters that are visually similar should be introduced well apart, for example n/h and g/y. In addition, the popping sounds, made without the voice /p/, /t/ and /k/ as in the words *pet, tin* and *kit,* are hard to hear at the beginning of words as the sound merges quickly with the following vowel. The voiced popping sounds /g/, /d/, as in *dog, bed* and *rid* may be difficult to identify at the end of words. Many children find it hard to say the sounds in words such as *sing,* where the **g** may be left off and *red,* which may be pronounced with a final /t/ sound.

Learning letters

When children are first learning about sounds and letters, mini-sessions that focus on one letter can be developed over several days. The following are some activities that could be included. To begin with, display books, cards and catalogues that have a particular letter and sound as a focus. For example, books with the letter **a** include *Pat the Cat* by Colin and Jacqui Hawkins, *The Cat in the Hat* by Dr Seuss, and *Angus and the Cat* by Marjorie Flack.

Many teachers collect jingles based on particular letters. These can be read aloud and the focus sound noted.

MAKING THE SOUND

- Show how the sound is made in the mouth. Find children's names and objects in the room that begin with the sound.
- Read aloud an alphabet book, either a big book or a smaller book. Point to the capital and lower case form of the letter. The children could trace the letter shapes in the air.
- Sing the alphabet song and point to the letters on an alphabet chart as the children sing.
- Tell children the name of the letter and the sound it can represent.

MAKING THE SOUND–LETTER LINK

- Write words that begin with the focus letter on the board underneath each other so the letter is clear, and ask children to identify the beginning letter.

> and
> ant
> apple
> Ann

- Many teachers make it explicit that the *letter* is written down and can be seen and named, and a *sound* is made in the mouth and can be heard. Spoken words are made up of sounds. Written words are made up of letters.

EXPLORING THE SOUND–LETTER LINKS

There are many ideas here for several sessions.
- Cut up an alphabet chart and place the letters on cards. In small groups, the children can place the letters in alphabetic order.
- Write words in a cut-out shape that begins with the focus letter. For example, words beginning with the letter **a** in an arrow shape.
- Make a chart of words that begin with the focus letter found in magazines and newspapers.
- Make the capital and lower case forms of the letter with plasticine or play dough.
- Invent alliteration tongue twisters: Alice's alligator has an appetite for alphabets.
- Create chants and rhymes around the focus letter.

What about high-frequency words?

Children need to build an ever-increasing set of high-frequency words – words that occur most regularly in reading and writing. High-frequency words are recognised automatically, by sight, and children do not have to sound or spell them out.

When children are beginning to read and write, knowledge of several high-frequency words helps them to quickly monitor the meaning in reading. They also need to be able to write a number of high-frequency words to be able to produce longer and more meaningful sentences.

The following is a beginning list of words the child may have learnt to read as an emergent reader.

[child's name], I, a, is, in, am, to, come, like, see, the, my. we, and, at, here, on, up, look, go, this, it, me (Clay 1993)

Opposite is a list of 100 high frequency words which are usually recognised by children in the first two years of school.

Many teachers use lists of high-frequency words as a pre-test to see how many words children can recognise. Words that require additional recognition practice can be written out on colored paper and displayed in various ways, for example attached to the floor as footprints to read or taped to the classroom word wall. Some teachers write a beginning list of words on a chart which is placed on the children's table. Some of the beginning high-frequency words can be written on cards and placed in tins on the writing table.

a	come	I	on	they
after	could	I'm	one	this
all	day	if	or	to
am	did	in	our	too
an	do	in	out	two
and	don't	is	over	up
are	for	it	play	us
as	from	like	put	was
asked	get	little	said	we
at	go	look	saw	went
away	going	make	see	were
back	had	man	she	what
be	has	mother	so	when
because	have	me	some	where
before	he	my	that	who
big	her	no	the	will
but	here	not	their	with
by	him	now	them	would
came	his	of	then	you
can	how	old	there	your

Word walls are an excellent idea for grouping high-frequency words. The words can be categorised alphabetically, and the teacher can add five or so new words each week. Children can read the words, and clap their hands or snap their fingers to the syllable beat as they read them aloud daily to increase their recall.

27 High-frequency words displayed for children to identify

CHAPTER FIVE

Assessing phonics
As/ses/sing pho/nics

The most effective way to assess children's understanding of phonics – the relationship between sounds and letters – is to assess their use of phonics in context within real literacy activities. When children are writing they are using their knowledge of sounds and letters. When they are reading, sounds and letters are one information source along with syntax, semantics and the visual layout of the text.

28 When children write, they are using their knowledge of sounds and letters

How do the children use phonics in writing?

There are several assessment procedures that can be used to monitor children's progress in using phonics in writing. Teachers can collect samples of children's writing and analyse them for knowledge of letters and sounds, and note particular features such as the use of high-frequency words.

Dictation can be given to explore how children are using phonics to problem solve. For example, a teacher asked the class to write a sentence she dictated: 'Today we had our photos taken.' This simple activity quickly showed what sounds and letters the children wrote with confidence.

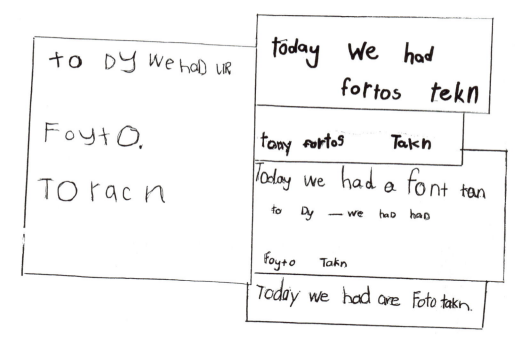

29 Simple dictation can quickly show how children are using phonics to solve problems.

How do the children use phonics in reading?

To assess children's use of phonics as an information source in reading, many teachers ask a child to read while they take a record of reading behavior. The child's miscue below signals the need to draw attention to the first letter of a word as an important strategy in reading.

✓   grub   ✓ ✓ ✓ ✓

Text: The caterpillar is on a leaf.

The first letter and sound is an important cue in reading, and regularly listening to children read provides ongoing information for assessment. Reading strategies teachers can watch for include self-correcting by checking letters and sounds, monitoring the relationship between letters and sounds, being able to differentiate between letters and words, and matching words one-to-one. Children also need to have at their fingertips important terminology such as first letter, last letter, beginning letter.

Focused assessment

There are times when teachers need to check to see what letters and sounds children know. At these times, a list of letters on a piece of cardboard with a cut-out frame covering all but one line of letters is a quick and practical way to assess a child's letter recognition. Children can be asked to identify the letter by name – aye, bee, cee – or they can be asked for the sounds – /a/, /b/, /c/. Children may be asked to identify the letters without a prompt for names and letters, and their preferred method of identifying the letters can then be noted. Sometimes assessment tasks that explore children's conscious attention to sound is important.

The following two assessment sheets can be used to assess a range of phonics knowledge.

Phonemic awareness assessment

This assessment procedure can be adapted to assess children's awareness of the spoken word, syllables, alliteration, rhyme and sound segmenting in words.

WORD

- Place a counter for each word you hear.

    Fay has five fantastic fish
    Correct response 5 counters

SYLLABLE

- Clap at each syllable or beat in a word.

    finger   fish   Fay
    Correct response
    2 claps   1 clap   1 clap

ALLITERATION

- Tell me what is the same about these words.

    four fingers five
    Correct response 'They begin with the /f/ sound.'
- Tell me the word that does not have the same first sound

    fish   fun   dog
    Correct response – dog.

RHYME

- Say a word that rhymes with these words

    fish   dish   ......
    Fay   say   ......

    Correct response any 'ish' word and any 'ay' 'eigh',' a-e' word or word with the long /a/ sound.

PHONEME

- What sounds do you hear in the word fish? Yes, f-i-sh
- What sounds do you hear in these words?

    fin   f-i-n
    five   f-I-v

Identifying sounds and letters

Cover the rows of letters so that only one row of letters shows. Ask children to identify the letters. They may identify the letter name or sound, or provide a word that begins with that sound.

A	Q	W	E	R	T
Y	U	I	C	O	P
F	L	K	J	H	G
D	S	Z	V	B	
	N	M	X		
m	n	b	c	a	
x	z	l	k	j	h
i	g	f	d	s	a
	p	o	u	y	g
	t	r	e	q	v	w

CHAPTER SIX

Summing up

Sum/ming up

Teachers draw on a range of practical ideas from different theories and experiences when teaching phonics. This is because there are always children who challenge our theories and make us rethink and review. Some children may appear passive and puzzling until we find ways to work with them. Relying on one narrow framework, one neat box, can limit our thinking and possibilities.

For many years phonics has been influenced by connectionist theories which have provided much useful information about phonemic awareness and the teaching of phonics. Connectionist theories provide clear examples of how spoken language can be explored by hearing words, syllables, rhyme and alliteration, and how sounds can be blended to make words. This theory does not consider the importance of social interaction in learning. In addition, programs based solely on connectionist theory can in fact be criticised for teaching children to be skilled workers with the code and not critical thinkers of what texts can mean.

Other theories and views of learning have influenced ways that phonics is taught. Cognitive psychology provides important strategies for using prior knowledge, memory and associations for building knowledge. Social constructivist theories reveal that language is embedded in culture and that culture is not just an overlay of thinking. Language and literacy is culturally and socially constructed and it mediates thinking. Poststructuralism as a theoretical tool highlights the importance of the construction of identity and how identity is continually being formed. Poststructuralism alerts teachers to be on guard and challenge practices that perpetuate narrow cultural stereotypes.

It is impossible to separate out literacy from the social and cultural worlds of children. The literacies used in communities and in everyday life can be the basis for developing meaningful explorations of the alphabetic principle. The connections made between community knowledge and school knowledge are central to this idea. This is more than the idea of taking children from where they are. The teacher has to seek out and understand different knowledge from within children's worlds and make connections between this and what's important in learning to read and write.

Children who are beginning to read and write vary considerably in what they already know about meaning making, forms and functions of written language. The teacher's scaffolding, modelling and explicit demonstrations will not resonate equally with each child's knowledge of how written language works. However:

> [I]f a teacher's demonstrating and highlighting are sufficiently holistic, that is, embedded in meaningful, social-communicative contexts, then it is possible to apply a single teaching event to varying individual problems they are on the verge of solving.

> (Richgels 1995: 108)

There is no doubt that the alphabetic code is important for children's literacy development. Finding new ways of exploring the code with children is promising and exciting.

30 Exploring how letters and sounds work

Phonics terminology

Phonics is instruction in the relationship between the sounds of language and the letters used to represent them. Phonics is one information source that helps children to identify printed words in reading quickly and accurately. Phonics helps children compose words in writing.

A letter is written. Letters are visual. We read and see letters. Sounds are spoken. Sounds are made in the mouth and are heard. Early readers and writers learn that spoken words have sounds, and written words have letters.

Orthography

Orthography is the spelling system of a language. In English there are 26 letters to represent the sounds. English spelling sometimes requires doubling consonants to represent different vowel sounds (*robed* and *robbed*).

Orthography is important in early literacy because the English language has common or likely sequences of letters in spelling. Common sequences of letters help make recognising and writing words quick and easy. For example, 'ant' and 'com' are common sequences within a word, but 'wgf' and 'qrs' are not.

Sounds and letters

There are consonant and vowel sounds in the English language. The consonant letter–phoneme correspondences in English are not as variable as are the vowel letter–phoneme correspondences.

Consonants

Table 1: Consonant letter-phoneme correspondences

	Grapheme	Examples
Single-letter/ single-sound	b	<u>b</u>at, ro<u>b</u>
	c	<u>c</u>at
	c	<u>c</u>ent, fa<u>c</u>e
	d	<u>d</u>oll, re<u>d</u>
	f	<u>f</u>at, i<u>f</u>
	g	<u>g</u>o, do<u>g</u>
	g	<u>g</u>em, pa<u>g</u>e
	h	<u>h</u>e
	j	<u>j</u>am
	k	<u>k</u>eep, see<u>k</u>
	l	<u>l</u>ight, coa<u>l</u>
	m	<u>m</u>e, a<u>m</u>
	n	<u>n</u>o, i<u>n</u>
	p	<u>p</u>ill, cu<u>p</u>
	r	<u>r</u>un, dea<u>r</u>
	s	<u>s</u>ay, bu<u>s</u>
	s	hi<u>s</u>
	s	<u>s</u>ure
	t	<u>t</u>ell, i<u>t</u>
	t	fu<u>t</u>ure
	v	<u>v</u>erb, lo<u>v</u>e
	w	<u>w</u>et
	x	<u>x</u>ylophone
	y	<u>y</u>es
	z	<u>z</u>eal, qui<u>z</u>
	z	a<u>z</u>ure
Double-letter/ single-sound	bb	e<u>bb</u>, ra<u>bb</u>it
	cc	a<u>cc</u>ount
	dd	a<u>dd</u>, la<u>dd</u>er
	ff	mu<u>ff</u>, mu<u>ff</u>in
	gg	e<u>gg</u>, nu<u>gg</u>et
	gg	exa<u>gg</u>erate
	ll	pu<u>ll</u>, ba<u>ll</u>oon
	mm	Gri<u>mm</u>, co<u>mm</u>on
	nn	i<u>nn</u>, ma<u>nn</u>er
	rr	bu<u>rr</u>, pa<u>rr</u>ot
	ss	lo<u>ss</u>, me<u>ss</u>age
	ss	i<u>ss</u>ue
	ss	s<u>ss</u>ors
	tt	mu<u>tt</u>, bo<u>tt</u>om
	zz	fu<u>zz</u>, da<u>zz</u>le

Consonant sounds

Consonant sounds are formed when there is an obstruction of air. The consonant sounds are divided into several different groups.

POPPING SOUNDS OR STOPS

These consonants are known as 'popping sounds' or stops. A stop is made by closing off the breath.

$$/p/, \ /b/, \ /t/, \ /d/, \ /c/, \ /g/$$

Some popping sounds are voiced and some are unvoiced. The consonant /g/ is voiced and made in the same place as /c/ which is unvoiced.

Table 2: Voiced and unvoiced popping sounds

	voiced	unvoiced
lips	/b/	/p/
front of mouth	/d/	/t/
back of mouth	/g/	/c/

LONG SOUNDS OR FRICATIVES

Long sounds or fricatives are produced when air is forced out in a long stream. Long sounds can be voiced or unvoiced.

Table 3: Voiced and unvoiced long sounds

	voiced	unvoiced
lips and teeth	/v/	/f/
teeth	/ð/ thy	/θ/ thigh
front of mouth	/z/	/s/
roof of mouth	/ž/ azure	/š/ sugar

COMBINATION SOUNDS OR AFFRICATIVES

Some consonants are produced when two sounds are combined or when air is forced through the nose or tongue. Affricatives are combination sounds where two sounds are combined like /ch/ as in chill and /j/ as in *Jill.* The 'ch' in *chill* is made up of ch = t plus sh.

NOSEY SOUNDS OR NASALS

These sounds are made by air forced into the nasal passages.
                        /m /, /n/ and /ng/

GLIDES

Glides occur when the sound seems to glide along in /y/ in *yes* and *yellow.*

LIQUIDS

These are long sounds: /r/ and /l/

UNUSUAL CONSONANT SOUNDS

The letter **c** may have a soft sound in *city* and *centimetre* or a hard sound in *cat* and *cup.*

The letter **g** may have a soft sound in *gym* and *gem* or a hard sound in *gate* and *gut.*

Table 4: Words with soft and hard g and c

g soft	c soft
geranium	centimetres
giraffe	cement
giant	Cinderella
gingerbread	city
gym	circle
g hard	**c hard**
gate	cat
goal	can
give	cup
go	cone
gun	cot

Vowels

Vowels are made in the mouth. There are no contact points between the lips, teeth and tongue.

VOWEL SOUNDS

The mouth takes up a different shape when vowel sounds are made, for example in these words:

> **a** in *apple*
> **ee** in *eat*
> **u** in *under*

For many vowel sounds there is not much movement in the mouth, for example:

> if eat apron

Table 5: Vowel sounds

Vowel phonemes	Key words
short /a/	<u>a</u>ct, c<u>a</u>t, b<u>a</u>ck
long /a/	<u>a</u>pe, b<u>ai</u>t, d<u>ay</u>
short /e/	<u>e</u>lk, b<u>e</u>t, d<u>e</u>ck
long /e/	<u>ea</u>t, b<u>ea</u>t, s<u>ee</u>
short /i/	<u>i</u>s, h<u>i</u>t, p<u>i</u>ck
long /i/	<u>i</u>ce, l<u>igh</u>t, b<u>uy</u>
short /o/	<u>o</u>x, c<u>o</u>t, d<u>o</u>ck
long /o/	<u>o</u>wn, c<u>oa</u>t, t<u>oe</u>
diphthong oi	<u>oi</u>l, c<u>oi</u>n, b<u>oy</u>
short /u/	<u>u</u>p, c<u>u</u>t, l<u>o</u>ve
long /u/	<u>u</u>se, c<u>u</u>te, f<u>ew</u>
short double o	b<u>oo</u>k, p<u>u</u>t
long double o	s<u>oo</u>n, m<u>o</u>ve, y<u>ou</u>
diphthong ou	<u>ou</u>t, cl<u>ou</u>d, c<u>ow</u>
vowel schwa	<u>a</u>bove, s<u>u</u>cceed,

There are 15 simple vowel sounds.

Table 6: Common vowel sounds

if	bite	tool
bet	beat	took
at	aid	bought law
hot	boat	out owl
up	use	boy oil

Some vowel sounds are known as short vowels and some are long vowels.

SHORT VOWELS

There are five short vowels. Short vowels in the middle of words are more difficult to distinguish than consonants.

    bat   be   bit   hot   but

LONG VOWELS

There are five long vowel sounds that often have the same sound as their name.

    aid   beat   bite   boat   use

ADDITIONAL VOWELS

There are three vowel sounds that are made high in the back of the mouth with the lips rounded.

    tool   took   bought

Two vowel sounds are close blends of two sounds. These vowels are called diphthongs.

    out   boy

THE SCHWA SOUND

The schwa sound is heard in *roses, omen* and *symbol* and occurs in an unstressed syllable. The schwa sound can be spelled in different ways. The schwa sound sounds a bit like a short /u/ sound. The sound is written in dictionaries like this ə.

Onset and rime

The following word families have similar rimes. Words with consonant blend onsets are in parentheses.

back	bake	day	cap	bug	bank	cot	Dick
Jack	cake	gay	gap	dug	rank	dot	kick
lack	fake	hay	lap	hug	sank	got	lick
pack	lake	lay	map	jug	tank	hot	nick
rack	make	may	nap	mug	(blank)	lot	pick
sack	rake	pay	rap	rug	(crank)	not	sick
tack	sake	ray	tap	tug	(drank)	pot	(brick)
(black)	take	say	(clap)	(chug)	(flank)	(blot)	(chick)
(crack)	wake	way	(flap)	(drug)	(frank)	(plot)	(click)
(shack)	(brake)	(clay)	(slap)	(plug)	(plank)	(shot)	(slick)
(slack)	(flake)	(play)	(snap)	(slug)	(prank)	(slot)	(stick)
(stack)	(shake)	(stray)	(strap)	(smug)	(spank)	(spot)	(thick)
(track)	(snake)	(tray)	(trap)	(snug)	(thank)	(trot)	(trick)

bag	bail	gain	bat	bump	can	came	
gag	fail	lain	cat	dump	Dan	dame	fill
lag	hail	main	fat	hump	fan	fame	hill
nag	mail	pain	hat	jump	man	game	kill
rag	nail	rain	mat	lump	pan	lame	mill
sag	pail	vain	pat	pump	ran	name	pill
tag	rail	(brain)	rat	(chump)	tan	same	will
wag	sail	(drain)	sat	(plump)	van	tame	(drill)
(brag)	tail	(grain)	(brat)	(slump)	(bran)	(blame)	(skill)
(drag)	(frail)	(plain)	(flat)	(stump)	(clan)	(flame)	(spill)
(flag)	(trail)	(train)	(scat)	(thump)	(plan)	(frame)	(still)

best	bet	bunk	bell	bit	dim	dear	bad
lest	get	dunk	fell	fit	him	fear	dad
nest	jet	hunk	sell	hit	Jim	hear	fad
pest	let	junk	tell	pit	rim	near	had
rest	met	sunk	well	sit	Tim	rear	lad
test	net	(drunk)	yell	wit	(brim)	tear	mad
vest	pet	(flunk)	(shell)	(flit)	(grim)	year	pad
zest	set	(skunk)	(smell)	(grit)	(slim)	(clear)	sad
(blest)	wet	(spunk)	(spell)	(slit)	(swim)	(smear)	(glad)
(crest)	(fret)	(trunk)		(split)	(trim)		

Blends, digraphs and diphthongs

When two or more letters are combined they are known as blends or letter clusters. Sequences of consonants are generally called *clusters* in linguistic writings and *blends* in reading instructional materials. Digraphs are one sound and can be consonant digraphs and vowel digraphs.

Blends

In a blend, the maximum number of consonants at the beginning of a syllable is three and the third letter is always 'r' or 'l', as in *stream, scrum* and *splurge*. Three consecutive consonant phonemes are usually regarded as the maximum length of a consonant blend in final as well as in initial position.

Consonant blends are usually grouped in two categories: those that occur at beginnings of single syllable words and those that occur at the end. There are some sequences of consonant sounds that never occur within the same syllable in English, such as 'bj' in *ob/ject*, 'zb' in *hus/band*, and 'vr' in *chev/ron*. Syllabic divisions automatically occur between them in multi-syllabic words.

Only three consonant blends occur regularly as initial and final blends. They are (1) 'sp' representing /sp/ as in *spell* and *grasp*; (2) 'sc' or 'sk' representing /sk/ as in *scale* and *ask*; and (3) 'st' representing /st/ as in *stage* and *rust*. All other blends may be identified predominantly with one position or the other. In a number of cases final blends are reversals of initial blends as are, for example, the initial and final blends in *broad/barb*, *flop/elf* and *drain/hard*.

Table 7: Consonant blends

	Grapheme	Examples
Two letters/	bl	<u>bl</u>ack
two sounds	br	<u>br</u>eak
(initial consonant	cl	<u>cl</u>ip
blends)	cr	<u>cr</u>ust
	dr	<u>dr</u>aw
	dw	<u>dw</u>ell
	fl	<u>fl</u>ood
	fr	<u>fr</u>ee
	gl	<u>gl</u>ass
	gl	<u>gl</u>ass

	Grapheme	Examples
	gl	glass
	pl	play
	pr	proud
	qu	queen
	sc	scare
	sk	skate
	sl	slow
	sm	small
	sn	snow
	sp	speech
	st	stop
	sv	svelte
	sw	swim
	tr	trip
	tw	twin
Two letters/ two sounds (final blend)	ct	sect
	ft	raft
	lb	bulb
	lc	talc
	ld	hold
	lf	self
	lk	bulk
	lm	helm
	ln	kiln
	lp	pulp
	lt	salt
	mp	jump
	nd	hand
	nk	pink
	nt	pant
	pt	rapt
	rb	barb
	rc	arc
	rd	board
	rf	scarf
	rg	berg
	rk	dark
	rl	curl

	Grapheme	Examples
	rm	fa<u>rm</u>
	rn	wa<u>rn</u>
	rp	ha<u>rp</u>
	rt	pa<u>rt</u>
	sk	ta<u>sk</u>
	sp	wa<u>sp</u>
	st	te<u>st</u>
Three letters/ three sounds (initial)	scr	<u>scr</u>eam, e<u>scr</u>ow
	spr	<u>spr</u>ing, o<u>spr</u>ey
	str	<u>str</u>ipe, fru<u>str</u>ate
Three letters/ three sounds (final)	mpt	pro<u>mpt</u>
	rld	wo<u>rld</u>
	rpt	exce<u>rpt</u>
	rst	fi<u>rst</u>

Table 8: Words with initial consonant blends

br	cr	dr	fr	gr	pr	st (tr)
brother	cry	dress	friend	grade	pretty	tree
bring	cross	drink	from	great	present	train
brought	crop	draw	front	ground	president	trip
brown	creek	dry	Friday	green	program	truly
brake	crowd	drive	fruit	grand-mother	print	trick
bread	cream	drop	fright	grass	produce	truck
bright	crack	dream	free	grand-father	prize	trade
bridge	crawl	drove	fresh	group	promise	trap
break	crib	drum	frog	grew	proud	track
brave	cried	drew	freeze	gray	product	true
brush	crumb	drill	frozen	grain	prepare	trail
branch	crown	drag	friendly	grab	protect	treat
brick	crow	drank	fry	grape	press	trim
broom	crook	drug	frost	grand	price	tramp

bl	cl	fl	pl	sl	sp	tr (st)
black	close	flower	play	sleep	spell	start
blue	clean	fly	place	sled	spend	stay
blow	class	floor	please	slid	spot	story
block	clothes	flag	plant	slate	speak	stop
bloom	climb	flew	plan	slip	spent	store
blew	club	flood	planes	slowly	sport	study
blanket	cloth	float	plenty	slave	speed	still
blood	cloud	flat	plain	slow	spoke	state
black-	clear	flour	plate	slipper	spirit	stand
board	clay		pleasant	slept	speech	stick
blossom	clothing	gl	plow	sleet	spoon	stock-
blind	clock	glad	player	sleepy	spear	ing
blame	climate	glass	planta-	slim	space	step
blizzard	clown	glove	tion	slick	spin	star
blaze			playmate			stood

sm	sn	sc	sk	sw	tw
small	snow	school	skate	swim	twelve
smoke	snake	scare	skin	sweet	twist
smell	snowball	scold	sky	swing	twent
smile	snail	scout	ski	sweater	twice
smart	snap	scream	skip	swan	twin
smooth	snug	school-	skirt	sweep	twig
smack	sneeze	house	skunk	swell	twinkle
		score			

DIGRAPHS

Digraphs are two letters that represent a single sound. They are combinations of consonants or vowels representing single phonemes that neither letter in the combination ordinarily represents alone.

Table 9: Consonant digraphs

	Grapheme	Examples
Two letters / one sound	ch	<u>ch</u>ild, ea<u>ch</u>
	ph	<u>ph</u>one, gra<u>ph</u>
	sh	<u>sh</u>ip, fi<u>sh</u>
	wh	<u>wh</u>ip,
	th	<u>th</u>in, bo<u>th</u>
	th	<u>th</u>en, ba<u>th</u>e

Table 10: Vowel digraphs

ai	<u>ai</u>m, p<u>ai</u>nt, ret<u>ai</u>n
ay	g<u>ay</u>, m<u>ay</u>onnaise
ea	<u>ea</u>t, p<u>ea</u>ce, t<u>ea</u> t<u>ea</u>cher
ee	<u>ee</u>k, r<u>ee</u>l, s<u>ee</u>, n<u>ee</u>dle
oa	<u>oa</u>ts, r<u>oa</u>d, t<u>oa</u>ster

DIPHTHONGS

Diphthongs are vowels that make two sounds in the mouth.

<u>oi</u>l   t<u>oy</u>

Table 11: Diphthongs, blends and digraphs

	Refers to	Type of sound	Sounds	Letters	Examples
diphthong	sound	vowel	2	1 or 2	b<u>oy</u> c<u>i</u>der
blend	sound	consonant	2 or 3	2 or 3	<u>fl</u>ip <u>str</u>ing
digraph	spelling	vowel or consonant	1	2	<u>th</u>ing k<u>ee</u>p

VOWEL SOUNDS AFFECTED BY R

Some vowel sounds are affected by **r** and the sound of the vowel changes.

Table 12: Vowel sounds affected by *r*

ar	er	or	ir
car	her	for	bird
farm	term	horse	girl
part	under	corn	third

Table 13 Some of the more common 'vowel –r' words

-ar		*-er*	*-or*
car	yard	her	for
farm	park	person	corn
march	card	term	storm
part	far	serve	horn
star	smart	ever	short
dark	arm	certain	north
hard	bark	berth	horse
barn	tar	herd	corner
start	spark	under	form

VOWELS AFFECTED BY L, LL, W AND U

In many words the vowels can be affected by **l**, **ll**, **w** and **u**.

Table 14: Vowels affected by *l, ll, w* and *u*

alk	all	aw	au
talk	tall	saw	haul
walk	fall	draw	because

THE OO SOUNDS

Most oo words are pronounced in one of two ways
> The sound heard in *boot* and *boo*.
> The sound heard in *book* and *foot*.
> The words *blood/flood* and *door/floor* are exceptions.

Syllables

There are as many syllables in a word as there are vowel *sounds*. Views on syllabification can vary. The following generalisations are based on Heilman 1976.

Syllables divide between double consonants, or between two consonants.

hap pen	can non	sud den	ves sel	vol ley
bas ket	tar get	cin der	har bor	tim ber
don key	pic nic	gar den	lad der	let ter

A single consonant between vowels usually goes with the second vowel.

fa mous	ho tel	di rect	ti ger	ce ment	pu pil
ea ger	wa ter	po lice	lo cate	va cant	spi der
be gin	fi nal	be fore	pi lot	li bel	sto ry

(The previous two generalisations are often combined: Divide *between* two consonants and in *front* of one.)

As a general rule, do not divide consonant digraphs *(ch, th,* etc) and consonant blends.

teach er	weath er	ma chine	se cret	a gree
broth er	preach er	ath lete	coun try	cel e brate

The word endings -ble, -cle, -dle, -gle, -kle, -ple, -tle, -zle constitute the final syllable.

mar ble	mus cle	han dle	sin gle	an kle	tem ple
ket tle	puz zle	no ble	pur ple	bat tle	bu gle

Structural analysis

Structural analysis involves the use of structural changes to a base word. Structural analysis includes adding inflectional endings (-s, -ed, -ing), prefixes and suffixes (pre-, un-, -less) and compound words.

Words ending with e

'Drop final e before adding a suffix beginning with a vowel.'

	+ed	+ing	+er	+est
bake	baked	baking	baker	
pale			paler	palest
late			later	latest

Doubling final consonants

Words that contain *one vowel* and end with a *single consonant* usually double that consonant before adding an ending beginning with a vowel.

big   bigger   biggest

Contractions

In oral language, children both use and understand contractions. In reading they need to learn the visual patterns involved and that a contraction:

- is a single word that results from combining two or more words
- omits one or more letters found in these words
- contains an apostrophe inserted where a letter or letters have been omitted
- carries the same meaning as the long form it represents but has its own pronunciation

Words	Contractions	Words	Contractions
I am	I'm	can not	can't
you are	you're	does not	doesn't
it is	it's	was not	wasn't
I have	I've	would not	wouldn't
you have	you've	could not	couldn't
they have	they've	should not	shouldn't

Compound words

Compound words are made by combining two words to make a different word, for example:

    some + thing = something
    some + one = someone
    some + time = sometime
    (schoolhouse, barnyard, football, birdhouse,
    firefighter, etc)

References

Adams, M. 1990. *Beginning to Read: Thinking and Learning about Print*. Cambridge MA: Massachusetts Institute of Technology.

Baumann, J., Hoffmann, J., Moon, J. & Duffy-Hester, A. 1998. 'Where are teachers' voices in the phonics/whole language debate? Results from a survey of U.S. elementary classroom teachers'. *The Reading Teacher*, 51 (8), 636–50.

Clay, M. 1993. *Reading Recovery: A Guidebook for Teachers in Training*. Auckland: Heinemann Education.

Clay, M. M. 1979. *Reading: The Patterning of Complex Behaviour*. Exeter NH: Heinemann.

Crawford, P. 1995. 'Early literacy: Emerging perspectives'. *Journal of Research in Childhood Education* (10) 1, 71– 86.

Cunningham, P., Hall, D. & Defee, M. 1998. 'Non-ability grouped, multi-level instruction: Eight years later'. *The Reading Teacher* 51 (8), 636–50.

Cunningham, P. & Cunningham J. W. 1992. 'Making words: Enhancing the invented spelling-decoding connection'. *The Reading Teacher* (46), 106–15.

Cunningham, A. 1990. 'Explicit versus implicit instruction in phonemic awareness'. *Journal of Experimental Child Psychology* 50, 429–44.

Ehri, L. 1987. *Movement into Word Reading and Spelling*. Berkley CA: University of California Press.

Ehri, L. 1995. 'Phases of development in learning to read words by sight'. *Journal of Research in Reading* (18), 116–25.

Elkonin, D. R. 1973. 'U.S.S.R.' in *Comparative Reading*, ed. J. Downing. Greenwich CT: JAI Press.

Fountas, I. & Pinnell, G. 1996. *Guided Reading: Good First Teaching for All Children*, Portsmouth NH: Heinemann.

Gee, J. 1987. What is literacy? Paper presented at the Marlman Foundation Conference on Families and Literacy. Cambridge MA: Harvard Graduate School of Education.

Gee, J. 1990. *Social Linguistics and Literacies: Ideologies in Discourses.* Hampshire UK: Falmer Press.

Goswami, U. 1994. 'Onsets and rimes as functional units in reading', in *Literacy Acquisition and Social Context*, ed. E. Assink. London: Harvester Wheatsheaf.

Heilman, A. W. 1976. *Phonics in Proper Perspective*, 3rd edn. Columbus, Ohio: Merrill.

Hill, S. 1997. 'Perspectives on early literacy and home-school connections'. *Australian Journal of Language and Literacy* (20) 4, 263–79.

Hill, S. 1999. *Guided Reading*, Focus on Literacy, Melbourne: Eleanor Curtain.

Hill, S., Comber, B., Louden, W., Rivalland, J. & Reid, J. *100 Children go to School.* Canberra: Commonwealth of Australia

Ives, J. P., Bursuk, L. Z. & Ives, S. A. 1979. *Word Identification Techniques.* Chicago IL: Rand McNally.

Iversen, S. & Tunmer, W. 1993. 'Phonological processing skills and the Reading Recovery program'. *Journal of Educational Psychology* (85) 1, 112–26.

Luke, A. 1993. 'The social construction of literacy in the primary school', in *Literacy Learning and Teaching: Language as Social Practice in the Primary school*, ed. L. Unsworth. Melbourne: Macmillan Education.

Maclean, M., Bryant, P. & Bradley, L. 1987. 'Rhymes, nursery rhymes and reading in early childhood'. *Merill-Palmer Quarterly* (33), 255–81.

Manguel, A. 1996. A History of Reading. London: HarperCollins.

McGee, L. & Purcell-Gates, V. 1997. 'Conversations: So what's going on in research in emergent literacy?' *Reading Research Quarterly* (32) 3, 310-319.

Moustafa, M. 1997. *Beyond Traditional Phonics: Research Discoveries and Reading Instruction.* Portsmouth NH: Heinemann.

Purcell-Gates, V. 1995. *Other People's Words.* Cambridge MA: Harvard University Press.

Rogoff, B. 1990. *Apprenticeship in Thinking: Cognitive Development in Social Context.* New York NY: Oxford University Press.

Richgels, D., Poremba, K., & McGee, L. 1996. 'Kindergarteners talk about print: phonemic awareness in meaningful contexts'. *The Reading Teacher* (49) 2, 632–42.

Richgels, D. 1995. 'Invented spelling ability and printed word learning in kindergarten'. *Reading Research Quarterly* (30) 1, 96–109.

Shannon, P. 1990. *The Struggle to Continue: Progressive Reading Instruction in the United States.* Portsmouth NH: Heinemann.

Solsken, J. 1993. *Literacy, Gender and Work in Families and in Schools.* Norwood NJ: Ablex.

Snow, C., Burns, S and Griffin, P. (eds) 1998. *Preventing Reading Difficulties in Young Children.* Washington DC: National Academy Press.

Spalding, R. & Spalding, W. T. 1962. *The Writing Road to Reading.* New York: Morrow.

Stahl, S., Duffy-Hester, A. & Stahl, K. A. 1998. 'Everything you wanted to know about phonics but were afraid to ask'. *Reading Research Quarterly* (33) 3, 338–55.

Strickland, D. 1998. *Teaching Phonics today: A Primer for Educators.* Newark DE: International Reading Association.

Strickland, D. & Cullinan, B. 1990. Afterword in *Beginning to Read: Thinking and Learning about Print.* M. Adams. Cambridge MA: Massachusetts Institute of Technology.

Strickland, D. & Morrow, L. (eds) 1989. *Emerging Literacy: Young Children Learn to Read and Write.* Newark DE: International Reading Association.

Sulzby, E. 1985. 'Children's emergent reading of favourite story books: A developmental study'. *Reading Research Quarterly* (20), 548–81.

Taylor, D. 1998. *Beginning to Read and the Spin Doctors of Science: The Political Campaign to Change America's Mind about How Children Learn to Read.* Urbana IL: National Council of Teachers of English.

Teale, W. & Sulzby, E. (eds) 1986. *Emergent Literacy: Writing and Reading.* Norwood NJ: Ablex.

Tunmer, W., Herriman, M. & Nesdale, A 1988. 'Metalinguistic abilities and beginning reading'. *Reading Research Quarterly* (23), 134–58.

Vygotsky, L. S. 1978. *Mind in Society: The Development of Higher Psychological Processes.* Cambridge: Harvard University Press.

Yopp, H. K.1992. 'Developing phonemic awareness in young children'. *The Reading Teacher* (45) 9, 696–703.

Yopp, H. K. 1995. 'A test for assessing phonemic awareness in young children'. *The Reading Teacher* (49) 1, 20–9.

Yopp, H. K, & Singer, H. 1985. 'Towards and interactive reading instructional model' in *Theoretical Models and Processes of Reading,* eds H. Singer & M. Ruddell. Newark DE: International Reading Association.

Wilde, S. 1997. *What's a Schwa Sound Anyway? A Holistic Guide to Phonetics, Phonics and Spelling.* Portsmouth NH: Heinemann.

Index